The Witch Of Plum Hollow

You are holding a reproduction of an original work that is in the public domain in the United States of America, and possibly other countries. You may freely copy and distribute this work as no entity (individual or corporate) has a copyright on the body of the work. This book may contain prior copyright references, and library stamps (as most of these works were scanned from library copies). These have been scanned and retained as part of the historical artifact.

This book may have occasional imperfections such as missing or blurred pages, poor pictures, errant marks, etc. that were either part of the original artifact, or were introduced by the scanning process. We believe this work is culturally important, and despite the imperfections, have elected to bring it back into print as part of our continuing commitment to the preservation of printed works worldwide. We appreciate your understanding of the imperfections in the preservation process, and hope you enjoy this valuable book.

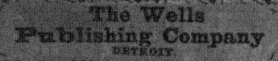
The Wells Publishing Company
DETROIT

THE WITCH OF PLUM HOLLOW

Romance

BY

Thos. W. H. Leavitt

THE WITCH

—OF—

PLUM HOLLOW

—BY—

THAD. W. H. LEAVITT.

✳✳✳✳

THE WELLS PUBLISHING COMPANY,
DETROIT, MICH.,
1892

Bancroft

812L.489
Y5

Copyright by Thad. W. H. Leavitt, 1892.

10168E

THE WITCH OF PLUM HOLLOW

BOOK I.

PART I.

CARL MARTYNE AT HOME.

It was a little brass plate bearing the modest inscription:

> CARL MARTYNE
> COUNSELLOR-AT-LAW

I gazed upon it with a fond pride, which years have not dimmed, and with a satisfaction which I have never experienced since that hour. It meant that I had passed my examination at the Albany Law School and had been admitted to the Bar of the Empire State. The surroundings were not luxurious, in truth, they were humble, if not positively shabby. The office was a seven by nine room on the fifth flat of a rambling structure, situated on Fourth Avenue, New York. The rent was only ten dollars per month and yet with my limited private income the problem which confronted me was, how I could pay the rent and manage to live, unless clients came to my assistance. A generous aunt had, in a moment of compassion, bequeathed to me a legacy of three hundred a year, but mindful of the follies of youth, had so arranged the gift that under no circumstances could I touch the principal. To quote her own words, "That, at least, is safe."

By the aid of teaching and pinching, principally pinching, I had worked my way through the law school, graduating as a plodder, and in no sense in a brilliant manner. People predicted my success because I was always self-possessed; critics said, cool and calculating.

Gazing upon the brass plate, ambition and pride seized upon me. I saw fat clients mounting the stairs and enquiring eagerly for the rising young barrister, Carl Martyne. The dingy office expanded into palatial chambers in a marble block on Broadway, with briefs and fees and an imposing bank account. Then I softly closed the door, and for the hundredth time arranged and re-arranged the blank deeds, wills and mortgages on my desk, so that my first client must be impressed with the value of my time and the press of business which demanded my unwearied attention. I cautiously locked the door, took from a tin box a small spirit lamp, lit it, and hung above the flame a miniature pail. These proceedings signified simply "coffee." With a penny bun I completed my breakfast. My matutinal repast over, I raised the window, aired the room and waited for a client. Where he was to come from I had not the most remote idea. Contrary to the advice of my rural friends at Penn Yann I had plunged into the metropolis without even a letter of introduction to a single citizen. Carl Martyne had faith in the future, particularly his own future. I then waited; yes, waited weeks and months. Day by day my resources diminished. Long since I had bought a second-hand rug, given up my sleeping-room on Sixth Avenue and boarded myself. A couch in the office, which was covered with horse-hair, furnished a substitute for a bed. The fiend who constructed that couch will have much to answer for in the future. By placing two chairs in front of the couch I managed to cling to its slippery surface while awake. A copy of Blackstone with an old coat served for a pillow. It was during the rare intervals when I slept that the trouble commenced. It not only commenced, but continued with a regularity which was mathematical in its precision. Once I dozed off I slipped first from my side on to my back and then began my descent by imperceptible gradations to the floor. The dreams which followed: I was being carried by an irresistible current down the Niagara River, I reached the rapids, the velocity constantly increased, I swept by Goat Island, clutching at the overhanging branches, the roar of the cataract resounded in my ears (it was but the creaking of the chairs). Then came the fatal plunge, not into the Whirlpool Rapids, but plump on to the floor. Half asleep I scrambled back to my bed of torture, lamenting the fate of a lawyer without clients, and again closed my eyes. In two minutes I was in a balloon, ten thousand feet above the earth; the balloon was leaking; I could distinctly hear the hissing gas as it escaped (it was the buttons on my coat scratching on the horse-hair) for I had by experience learned that in a night shirt I could not hang on when wide awake. Then the balloon began to sink, I held my breath and clutched the ballast, which I in vain attempted to cast overboard.

As I swept toward the earth I abandoned hope, burst into a cry of agony, and once more found myself on the floor. Not even De Quincey, in his wildest dreams, when under the influence of the potent poppy, created greater horrors than was born of that horse-hair couch. Idleness by day and nightmare by night combined to produce a state of coma in my intellectual faculties. I could not read. Carl Martyne was rapidly losing faith in himself.

One sultry afternoon, as I sat listlessly gazing out of my window, I was startled to my feet by hearing at my elbow a mellow voice repeating "Martyne, Martyne," with the accent on the last syllable. Turning suddenly, I found myself face to face with a little old man, dressed in a costume which might have come over in the Mayflower. In his left hand he held a knitted cap, in his right a number of faded papers, while under his arm he carried a rusty iron box.

My heart gave a great thump.

Was it a case at last?

Then I asked my visitor to be seated. I noted that his head was bald, save a fringe of white hair which ran, like a great ruff, around the base of the skull and was continued by a bushy fringe of beard under the chin. His upper lip and his ruddy cheeks were clean shaven. For some minutes he spoke not a word, while his keen blue eyes surveyed me carefully from head to foot. It was not a stare but simply a weighing-up. Instinctively I felt that all depended upon my quietly submitting to the scrutiny. By almost imperceptible degrees the corners of his mouth widened and a smile crept over his face, which was now a picture of good humor and complaisant satisfaction.

I ventured to enquire, "Is there anything which I can do for you?"

His reply was, "You are Martyne, Carl Martyne?"

"Yes, that is my name."

"Of French origin?" he queried.

"I believe so."

"I have been looking for you," he said. Then he pulled his chair up to the desk and began slowly untying the faded tape which held the bundle of papers.

I am not of an imaginative turn of mind, yet I felt that an atmosphere of the past was gradually diffusing itself through the room. As my visitor slowly unfolded the musty parchments, quaint with leaden seals and faded blue ribbons, I saw, rising before me and peopling the shabby little office, the stately cavaliers of the colonial age, the pilgrims and puritans—the woman upon whose breast blazed the "Scarlet Letter," by whose side gamboled little Pearl.

The rusty iron box, resting on the table near at hand, exhaled a breath born of Mother Earth, in whose lap it must have long been buried. Its sides were coated with a green mould, which hung in little patches, and at times they seemed to wink at me and whisper, "We hide a secret."

My curoisity was aroused to the highest pitch, and yet a feeling possessed me that what was taking place did not belong to the unexpected, but that in some way, I knew not how, my future was associated with these musty papers and the iron box. This was all the more remarkable as the man before me was a stranger. I had never before met such a type. Strive as I might I could not divest myself of the impression that he belonged to the remote past and consequently might suddenly vanish; or that through some mysterious oversight he had been forgotten by Old Father Time. He could not have died, for there he was at my side, hale, hearty and smiling. His age I could not guess. Judging by his hair, which was of that peculiar whiteness and fineness found only in extreme old age, he might have seen a century. The tint in his cheeks, the smile on his lips, the brightness of his blue eyes, which sparkled and twinkled, said this man is in the prime of life.

Having arranged the papers to his satisfaction, he drew a key from his pocket and fitted it in the lock of the box. Then he broke the silence, saying in a mellow, liquid tone, "So you are Carl Martyne."

I nodded assent.

"My name," he continued, "is Billa La Rue. I am of French origin, though English born and English bred. Your name, Martyne, indicates a similar origin. I want some business done by a lawyer and I have selected you. Will you take the case?"

"I shall only be too happy to do so, Mr. La Rue," I answered.

So critical was my financial position at that moment that I would have boldly entered into a legal dispute with the Chief Justice of the Supreme Court at Washington, or the dignitary on the Wool Sack at Westminster.

"It will take time," said La Rue, "and perhaps you can't spare it," glancing nervously at the dummy papers scattered over my desk. "Innocent soul," I murmured to myself, "They no more represent cases, than Carl Martyne represents capital."

La Rue heaved a sigh of relief, and pointing to the parchments, said, "These are the title deeds and grants from the Crown for my property, but other people are in possession, and what can I do? I have been absent such a long, long time." Then he folded his hands and looked at me in a way which was pathetic in its trust and simplicity. For a minute I waited for an explanation, but as it never came I took up the parchments and soon discovered that they were chronologically arranged. The first was a proclamation issued in 1783 by the Commander-in-Chief of His Majesty in British North America, to the United Empire Loyalists, offering them an asylum in Canada. Then followed an Order-in-Council setting apart certain public lands for distribution. These documents were followed by a series of letters, written in reply to an application for a large tract of land situated in the district of Johnstown, Upper Canada, made by Billa La Rue, an United Empire Loyalist. From these letters I gathered La Rue had, at a very early date, settled in the colony of Massachusetts, from which place he had been driven by the revolutionists of 1776, abandoning in his flight a very valuable estate, which was subsequently confiscated by the continental authorities. The last document was a deed for the grant of land, with an immense leaden seal, to which was attached a broad blue ribbon. The deed conveyed two thousand acres of land, and from the metes and boundaries I learned that the tract fronted upon the River St. Lawrence, but as my knowledge of early Canadian geography was limited to a perusal of Parkman's account of the tragic fate of the Jesuits on the shores of Lake Huron, I was unable to give even a guess as to the locality of the grant.

My lack of equipment for the task did not deter me from entering upon the case. Impecuniosity is reckless and hunger an imperative master. I possessed both in an eminent degree. As my client vouchsafed no further information, I proceeded to question him.

"These documents are unquestionably genuine, Mr. La Rue, but where is the missing link which connects you with the claim. Are you the heir-at-law, and are you certain that the original Billa La Rue did not alienate the estate or bequeath it to some person at the time of his death, which must have occurred a century since?"

"It is mine, mine, mine—all mine," murmured the enigma before me.

"Can you prove it?"

"That is for you to do," he answered, "what is the use of a lawyer if he can't prove things?"

"True," I replied, "but you must give me a statement of your claim, the data upon which it is based; and a geneological synopsis of your descent from the original Billa La Rue."

"You must find it," was the simple and laconic answer.

He then unlocked the iron box and disclosed the contents to view. It was full of of old gold coins from the French mint, issued long ere the first empire had been dreamed of, much less consummated by the daring Corsican.

"There," said La Rue, "is the pay for your services. Go to Canada and find what I want."

He took up the knitted cap, gave me his hand and in a moment was gone. I sat as one in a dream, then I rushed into the corridor only to see the car of the elevator rapidly descending. Down the stairs I darted, determined to overtake my client and obtain from him, at least, his address. I was doomed to disappointment. The car was empty and La Rue had disappeared from sight. Up and down the street surged the every-day throng, but nowhere could I catch a view of a form which in the slightest degree resembled that of my first client. Suddenly remembering that in my hurry I had left my office door open with the box of gold exposed, I as hurriedly mounted the stairs again. I should not have been surprised had I found that the parchments and gold had, in my absence, disappeared by following my mysterious client, but there they were as I had left them. Carefully locking the door I poured the gold upon the table. Counting it, I found that it consisted of 332 pieces, all of the same mint. The value I did not know as I had never before seen similar coins. After carefully arranging and depositing the parchments in my desk, I replaced the gold in the box and in so doing made the discovery that the box had been constructed so as to hold precisely 333 coins and therefore that one coin was missing. Perhaps La Rue had retained it as a momento of the past, or to confront me with upon some future occasion. I took the box to Wall Street for the purpose of ascertaining the value of the coins and also to deposit them in a place of safety. I decided upon the agency of the Bank of Montreal at No. 59, being influenced in my choice by the fact that Montreal was a French-Canadian city and that in consequence the officials would in all probability possess a knowledge of the ancient coins. Enquiring the value of one of the pieces from the cashier, he confessed that he was as ignorant as myself, remarking that I could sell it by weight. Accepting his advice I disposed of the entire sum, except one coin, which I retained. Placing the proceeds on deposit as a trust fund, *re* the Billa La Rue case, I returned to my office and for hours pondered over the eventful circumstances of the day. I carefully re-examined the papers, but discovered no new facts. The iron box contained no clue which would assist in solving the mystery. That it had been buried for many years, the rust and the earth clinging to its sides demonstrated. I finally decided that my client must be a lineal descendant of the original Billa La Rue, who, for some unknown reason, had recently come into possession of the manuscripts and the box, upon which he founded his claim. It was evidently my duty in the premises to ascertain the location of the ancient district of Johnstown, and to search the records in the Registry Office, and, if necessary, the archives at Toronto and Ottawa, in the hope of discovering a clue which would substantiate my client's claim. Procuring a map of the Province of Ontario, I carefully traced the country bordering upon the St. Lawrence River, but found no mention of Johnstown District. Finally I decided that the most expeditious way to set the question at rest, was to proceed to Canada at once. My preparations were soon made. Paying my rent for three months in advance and securing the services of a youth as office boy, to explain to La Rue, when next he called, where I was, I departed. The next morning found me at Kingston, an atiquated Canadian city situated at the foot of Lake Ontario. A hurried inquiry at the land office demonstrated that my route had been well chosen. From the Deputy Registrar I learned that the old Johnstown District had long since been replaced by counties, of which Leeds and Grenville now covered the greater portion of that ancient territory. He advised me to proceed to Gananoque, where, no doubt, I should be able to obtain the desired information relative to the location of the La Rue estate. From Kingston I sailed on a small steamer through the Thousand Islands. The summer cottages and palatial residences, which dotted the islands on the American side, filled me with astonishment, while the sylvan beauty of the Canadian waters, where each islet remained in a state of nature, produced a contrast full of picturesque and placid beauty. During the past twenty-four hours my mind had been constantly peopled with images of the colonial past. I had grown to look upon the Canadian frontier as a relic of the age when the intrepid missionaries and voyageurs had begun the exploration, from Tadousac and Ville Marie, of the North American continent.

At Gananoque I ascertained that many years ago a mill had been built, about sixteen miles east, on the bank of the St. Lawrence, where a small stream falls into the river, and that at the present time the place is known as La Rue's Mills. This was all that I could learn. Leaving my baggage at the comfortable hotel with the genial Irish proprietor, McCarney, I determined to proceed on foot, making inquiries along the route. Taking the river road the next morning I found that I entered upon a scene of enchantment. To the south I caught, through openings in the pines and low bushes, vistas of river and islands stretching away to the American shore. The background, at the north, was a range of low-lying hills, clothed with tangled masses of shrubbery and crowned with sentinel hemlocks whose topmost bows nodded to me a welcome. They seemed to know that I came from a great city, full of dust and heat, and stretched forth their long arms as if to fold me in the embrace of Mother Nature. Evening found me in front of a substantial block-house, evidently a relic of the early past. At the door sat a woman whose round jolly face was the picture of good nature. My request for a night's shelter met with a cordial "Yes." After a substantial supper I lit my cigar and entered upon conversation with my hostess, whom I found seated beneath a Lombardy poplar in front of the house. From her I learned that these trees were originally planted by the French voyageurs all the way from Quebec to the Straits of Mackinac, to mark their camping posts. Good fellowship was at once established, for she drew from a box a churchwarden, the smoke of which soon blended with that of my cigar and floated lazily out upon the river. I produced a pocket flask and said, "Will you join me in a glass?" Her small eyes rested upon the case with a complacency which said, "It will complete my happiness." Peeping cautiously about, to see that her daughter was not visible, she grasped the flask and drank a potion commensurate with her bulk, but out of all proportion to the size of the bottle. Reluctantly she returned it, as if loth to part with so dear a friend. I felt that my offering had found the way to her heart. She closed her eyes for a few minutes, folded her hands. I thought she had fallen asleep, but such was not the case.

She opened the conversation by saying, "You are a Yankee?"

"Yes," I replied.

"Where were you born?"

"At Penn Yann."

"How old are you?"

"Twenty-five."

Then her loquacity burst all the barriers of restraint. She ran on and on with questions and queries, remarks and comments, opinions and conclusions, intermingled with flashes and sallies of Irish wit which left me in a half dazed condition. She waited not for answers; with the sound of her own voice she was supremely content. She was Irish. "Irish to the backbone" was her phrase. As she rambled from the County Down to St. Patrick's Day in the Morning, I discovered that she possessed, in addition to an imagination almost boundless in the fertility of its resources, a fund of information and shrewd common sense rarely found in a woman in her position in life. She reminded me of a mountain torrent long pent up and then suddenly set free. She poured forth little bits of history, biography, local gossip mingled with sly allusions to scandals, which would have made her fortune as a story teller in the *New York Weekly*. She only paused when completely out of breath.

Seizing my opportunity, I asked if she knew a place called La Rue's Mills.

The volubility which had excited my admiration, suddenly disappeared. The confidential glance was replaced by a look of extreme caution bordering upon distrust, if not suspicion. As a final resort I drew upon the consolation devoutly wished for, the pocket companion. The temptation was two powerful for resistance. For the second time she placed it to her lips and drained it of the last drop. Then I proceeded boldly by enquiring, " What do you think I am looking for?"

"The gold," she answered.

Up came the iron box and its contents before my mental vision. Yet I decided to give her no clue to my secret, but extract from her all information in her possession.

"It would be a fine thing to get hold of," I whispered, making a leap in the dark.

"Yes; but it will never be found," she replied.

"Why?" I inquired.

"Because it is guarded," she said in a stage whisper.

"Who guards it?"

"Oh! you know," she said, glancing at me with a suspicious look.

"Who?" I repeated.

"Old Billa himself," she answered, at the same time glancing nervously around, as if expecting the old man to suddenly appear at the mention of his own name.

"Do you know where it is?" I asked boldly.

"No," she answered sadly, "not for a certainty, but I have a good idea. But its no use; he won't part with it, and you may as well go home."

Beyond that statement she would not go, being no doubt influenced by the fear that I might secure the treasure.

In the course of the evening I obtained the following facts: At the time of the Revolutionary War, Billa La Rue had obtained a large grant of land from the Crown, the western boundary of the estate being within half a mile of the spot where I was sitting. On the estate was a small creek which emptied into the St. Lawrence. On this creek Billa had built one of the first grist mills erected in the Johnstown District. A dam had been thrown across a narrow ravine which had created an artificial lake nearly ten miles in length, thus furnishing plenty of water for motive power. La Rue, who must have been a man of great energy and possessed of a deep love for the comforts of civilization, had also built for himself a house which was a marvel in the days of the universal log cabin. It was a large rambling two and a half story frame building with a steep roof, and yet remained in an excellent state of preservation. By some means he had succeeded in obtaining a supply of apple, chestnut, sweet and English walnut trees, thus transforming the Canadian forest into an English homestead. Grapes and small fruits were also obtained and planted in the ravines, the hills to the north being left in a state of nature, thus furnishing a shelter which enabled him to raise fruit, which in the open could not have withstood the rigours of the Canadian winter. My informant, when a little girl, had been the playmate of Sarah, a stepdaughter of La Rue, he having married a widow late in life, with whom he lived for many years upon terms the reverse of amicable. During the war of

1812-15, La Rue had built several small rifle pits on his estate upon the banks of the river. These pits were garrisoned by red coats, who guarded the batteaux engaged in transporting provisions and munitions of war from Montreal to Little York. Long ere his death he was known to be a wealthy man, and was reputed to have his savings all in gold, but where they were concealed not even his wife had been able to discover. At his decease the estate fell into his wife's possession. She disposed of all the land with the exception of a few acres upon which the homestead stood. From that hour until the day of her death she and her daughter devoted all their time and energies to a search for the hidden gold. Not a brass farthing was ever found. Gradually there grew up in the neighborhood the belief that the old La Rue house was haunted by its former owner, whose spirit returned nightly to guard the hiding place. This legend did not deter the widow and Sarah. They dug up the cellar bottom, pried off the oak wainscotting of every room in the house, undermined the great chimney until it fell in ruins at their feet. Finding no reward within doors they resorted to the garden, which they dug over and over again. Not content they even pried into the tomb in which La Rue's remains had been buried, only to meet with disappointment. Then the public took up the search and continued it for many years with a like result. I had been assigned by my fat hostess to the ranks of the treasure-seekers. I assured her that I had never before heard of the hidden gold. She listened to me with a smile of incredulity which spoke volumes of doubt.

When I retired to my chamber I fell into a reverie.

I had become so accustomed, during the past few days, to the unexpected, if not the mysterious, that no discovery, however startling, would have surprised me.

The questions which confronted me were:—Who was my client? What was his relation to Billa La Rue, the elder? Had he ever been in Canada, and, if so, had he visited the homestead, and for what purpose?

That he was unknown to my hostess was beyond a doubt. Where did that old gold come from and where did he obtain possession of the original papers and deeds? To none of these queries could I find a reasonable answer. The next morning I hastened to pay a visit to the seat of the mystery, though with no hopes of securing any new facts relative to the case. I was convinced that the property, which had for nearly one hundred years been alienated from the La Rue family, could not be recovered by my client. Possession had long since quieted any flaw which might have originally existed in the title. At the mouth of La Rue's creek I found a man fishing for cat-fish, from whom I learned that the original mill had been built back about a quarter of a mile from the river. The house on the hill had been the home of La Rue, but nothing remained of the original structure save the frame work which was of solid oak. I found where the old mill had been built a few foundation stones, some remnants of machinery and the ruins of the original dam. The impression suddenly came upon me that I should visit the tomb of La Rue. Wending my way back to the mouth of the creek, from the fisherman I ascertained the location of the last resting-place of the founder of the settlement. My informant pointed up through the orchard to a narrow gorge, which stretched away like an avenue between the hills clothed with a thick growth of pines. As I picked my way through the narrow defile a feeling of sadness crept over me, combined with the sensations which I had felt when poring over the musty parchments in New York. Under a wide-spreading chestnut tree, to which clung an enormous grapevine, I came suddenly upon a great marble slab supported at each end by granite pillars raising the slab about two feet from the ground. On every side the grass grew in tangled masses, interwoven with struggling shrubs and golden rod. Perched upon the slab was a diminutive girl, with bare feet and legs red with scratches from briars. She was swinging her legs backwards and forwards, singing at the same time snatches of song in a treble, piping voice.

Her eyes were nearly round and of a liquid blue. Her dress, a shabby bit of calico, hanging in shreds and tatters. The little hands were brown as berries. On her head no covering save a tangled mass of flaxen hair which fell in great masses to her waist. Unconscious of my presence she sat upon the tomb of Billa La Rue, the embodiment of life and mirth, singing over decay and death. Smiles flitted over her face and wreathed her red lips. Her songs floated down the glade and sank to rest amid the rustle of the overhanging pines. Though I had not uttered a word she suddenly paused, looked up, and discovered me.

As I came forward and said "Good morning, my little girl of the wood," she nodded her head and did not attempt to run away as I had expected. Then I took a seat by her side. The place was so lonely that I much marvelled at her presence amongst the tombstones, several of which were scattered around, but not one upright. They were lying at all angles, as if Time had touched them with his dexter finger in mockery of man's attempt to perpetuate the names of those who had passed over the Great Divide.

"What are you doing here?" I inquired.

"Waiting for him to come back," she answered.

Then she cried out is childish glee, "There's Chitter."

I looked in vain for some person to appear, and then said, "Who is Chitter, and where is he?"

"You don't know Chitter, why Chitter is a squirrel, there, there," pointing to a half-fallen tombstone, upon which Chitter sat, evidently eyeing me with distrust.

"You go over there," said my little friend, pointing to a mound much resembling a grave. I complied. Then Chitter, by spasmodic quirps and jerks, advances and retreats, gradually came nearer and finally perched on the tomb beside the little girl, where he was rewarded with a crust of bread which was taken from a very dirty rag. Chitter ran gaily away and I took his place.

"Chitter," said my little friend, "has got a wife and family. Chitter has gone home to tell his wife that I'm here."

We waited a few minutes when Chitter's wife appeared and again I was ordered to return to my seat on the old neglected grave. Rosa (that was the wife's name) came frisking up to her child-friend but the cares of a family soon called her away.

After her departure I inquired about the family and

was told, with the greatest gravity, "That there were two of the cutest little baby squirrels you ever set your eyes on."

"Let us go and visit them," I proposed.

"No, you're a stranger, but if you stay until they grow up I'll make you acquainted," was the response.

I then inquired the name of my new found friend.

"Rue," was the answer.

"Rue what?"

"Rue Jahns."

"Where do you live?"

"At the p'int."

"Where is that?

"Don't you know the p'int? You must be a green-norn."

To this impeachment I assented, and then inquired, "How it happened that she knew Chitter and Rosa?"

"Oh! I run away every day, father never says a word, but sometimes mother tans me."

"What will she say to-day?"

"She wont know it. She's gone to Brock'ill to sell taters and cowcumbers and garden sass. Oh my! she's promised to buy me a picter. Yes, a real picter, not a black thing like we have in books, but a gen-u-er-ine picter, full of the most beau-ti-ful-er-ist colors, all pink and green, and, and you know." She stopped for want of breath.

At the mention of the picture her eyes flashed, she drew herself up to her full height and waved her chubby, dirty hands in the air.

At first sight I had thought her not more than

ten years of age, but now concluded that she must be twelve or thirteen, through very small for that age.

"How old are you?" I inquired.

"Don't know," in a tone of the utmost unconcern.

Then she grew silent; the long lashes fell upon her cheek. Finally in a shy half whisper full of doubt, she said, "Can you keep a secret?"

"Yes."

"You won't tell?"

"No."

"Hope to die in a minute—to drop stone dead and die and go to "——

"Stop," I exclaimed. "I won't tell."

"I guess you won't," she said, very slowly, as if debating my veracity in her own mind, and then suddenly, "You don't know mother anyway and father wouldn't care."

She slid down from her perch on the tomb, dropped on her knees and crawled beneath the great slab. When she emerged she held in her hand a little roll which she clutched with the tenacity born of intense love. She peeped about with a frightened look and then, making a table of the slab, she carefully unrolled the parcel. I saw at a glance that it consisted of a number of pieces of birch bark, the edges of which were ragged and dirty. Picking up four little stones she unrolled the outer piece of bark, taking care that I did not see the inner surface.

"Now shut your eyes," she said, "and no peeking."

I shut my eyes.

"Open," she cried.

Then I looked. Spread out on the slab was the

piece of birch bark with a little stone on each corner to prevent it from curling up. On the bark was a painting, or more properly, a sketch. I am not an artist, but I must confess that I opened my eyes with astonishment. I knew that the artist stood beside me. An artist with dirty hands and feet, scratched legs and a tattered dress. Impulsively I stooped down, seized her in my arms and kissed each dirty cheek. A frightened look came into her eyes, then she put her arms about my neck and began to sob. She was crying for joy, not sorrow. As she brushed away the tears, she whispered with a pathetic sigh, "Now I know you won't tell."

I placed her on the ground and one by one we examined her treasures.

They were sketches of the scene where we stood. The great chestnut tree, Chitter and Rosa, the pines with their cones strewn beneath, wild flowers struggling into the sunlight through the tangled grasses, a glimpse of the river with the islands beyond, the ravine with its babbling brook. In each sketch crude attempts at coloring had been made. The drawing, though lacking in finish, was striking in its accuracy and realistic in the extreme. In some way, I know not how, this child-artist had caught the salient points of each scene depicted. The work was strong, natural, full of promise of great power, I believed genius. Chitter and Rosa were full of life. The leaves on the great chestnut rustled, the pines sighed and sang their everlasting requiem, the grasses grew, the flowers blossomed.

"Surely," said I to myself, "amid these pines and hills has been born a great artist, and she is my friend.

When I asked where she got her paints, she darted

under the great slab and came out with a ragged cotton handkerchief with a knot tied in each corner. From the corners she produced, in succession, a stumpy black lead pencil, which I noticed she had sharpened by gnawing off the wood with her little teeth; a cake of blueing, used in washing clothes; a spoonful of yellow ochre and some crude venetian red. With these materials, which she had picked up, she had created the wonderful "picters," as she called them.

"Where are your brushes?" I inquired.

She simply stared at me with a puzzled expression on her face.

"How do you put the paints on?" I continued.

"Oh! with my fingers."

Brushes were an unknown quantity with this artist.

We sat down on the slab and had a long talk. She had not shown her treasures to any person before. Last week she had hoed nine rows of cabbages for her mother under the promise that a real painted picture should be bought for her in Brock'ill. "The picture will come to-night." Then she clapped her hands in childish glee, stopped, and in grave tones said, "I won't hoe any more cabbages." At that moment I too hated cabbages.

A surprise awaited me. She climbed up on the slab and gazed long and anxiously up the ravine.

"Who are you looking for?" I queried.

"Grandpa."

"Where does he live?"

"Don't know."

"What does he do?"

"Don't do nothin'."

"What is his name?"

"Ain't got a name. I tell you he's my grandpa."

"Tell me all about him," I said.

"Well he comes out of the woods, he does, and sits down with me on this stone. This is his chestnut tree, and he planted all these posies (pointing to the golden rod), and these are his graves, and he says them that's buried ain't dead, but live awake, and, and he says the pine trees talk, only most folks can't tell what they say; but I can. Listen, don't you hear them whispering, paint, paint pretty picters; and he showed me that them cones are beautifuler than they look to you."

She ran and gathered some cones and pointed out their convolutions and the tints and gradations in color, for which she had no name, but she saw them all with the eye of an artist.

Then she sadly shook her head and said, "I'm afeard he has gone away with a nasty, dirty, iron box, and he'll get tired out, and get sick, and won't come back to see Rue any more."

My heart gave a bound. Grandpa and the iron box. Could it be that this child knew my first client?

Rue's blue eyes were full of great tears.

I had no time to question her. She uttered a sharp cry of pain and cried out, "There's Dan Polly, he's got a gun and he says he'll shoot Chitter and Rosa and the baby squirrels, but you won't let him, will you?"

"No, I won't let him."

She went out a little way to meet her enemy, who was a great, lumbering, callow youth. Dan looked surprised when he caught sight of me, but came shambling along, paying no attention to little Rue, whose flashing eyes betokened the fiery spirit burning within. Ere I could interfere, Dan raised the gun and levelled it at Chitter, who had returned and was sitting on a low branch of the chestnut. With a cry of rage and fury Rue sprang at the boy, throwing up her hands to protect her pet. I rushed at Dan and at that instant the gun was discharged. The next moment I struck the great lout and sent him sprawling on the grass. In the smoke and confusion I felt that the child must be killed. No; like a wildcat she rushed upon the prostrate boy. Her little fists struck him in the eyes, her little nails scratched his cheeks until the blood ran. I caught her in my arms. Dan scrambled to his feet and, with a bellow and a roar which I shall never forget, bolted down the ravine. I seized the gun and broke it in twain over a fallen tombstone.

Rue began to laugh and shout, "We've licked him, we've licked him." As she held up her hand I saw that the blood was running down her arm and trickling from her elbow.

"My dear Rue," I cried, "you have been shot." I seized her hand and saw that a single grain had passed completely through the palm.

She looked down and said, "Pshaw! I don't care, we've licked Dan Polly and smashed his gun."

Chitter gave a responsive chuckle in the top of the tree, to which he had run for safety.

I bound up the wound with my handkerchief. Rue crept under the slab and hid her art treasures. I took her by the hand and started for her home, which proved to be a mile away.

The cabin, for it could not be called a house, had been built from timbers which had washed upon the beach. It was not more than six feet in height and was banked with earth half way up to the eaves to keep out the intense cold of the Canadian winter. Attached to the main building was a diminutive structure, which Rue informed me was father's room. The door was open and we entered without any warning.

"That's mother," said Rue, pointing to a stalwart woman.

'Madam," said I, "your little girl has been wounded in the hand by the accidental discharge of a——"

I never finished the sentence.

Mrs. Jahns poured out upon Rue a flood of abuse which shocked me.

"It was all her fault. She should have been at home working in the garden. It's what comes from gadding around the woods."

Rue slipped quietly away into her father's room, from which there emerged a little wizened old man, whose watery eyes and trembling hands cried "Drink." His clothing was in the last stages, verging upon dissolution from his body. It might, for aught I knew, have formed part of the wardrobe of Rip Van Winkle when he fled from Gretchen. Listening to the clatter of Mrs. Jahn's tongue and gazing at Jahns I said to myself—The hero and the vixen of the Catskills have come to life again in Canada.

Madam Jahns continued the outpour of her wrath. Nothing but death will silence that tongue. While Jahns quietly asked what was the cause of the accident and the full extent of the injury. In my explanation I assumed the principal blame, ascribing it to my negligence in not forbidding the boy to shoot.

Jahns produced a few drops of brandy, with which we bound up the wound. Jahns impressed me in a peculiar manner. His brow was broad and furrowed with deep lines, his hands small and exquisitely shaped, in his very rags there lingered a far-off culture and refinement utterly at variance with his present surroundings and attire. How he could have married *that* woman was a mystery beyond my ken. His language proclaimed him an educated man, while the utter neglect in which Rue had grown up, for she had told me without a blush that she could not read or write, proved the depths to which the father had fallen. Momentarily Jahns casts furtive glances at his spouse, who busied herself with spasmodic outbreaks of vituperation, blended with lamentations which should rank with those of Jeremiah.

I knew that the moment I departed Jahns and Rue would fall heirs to a lecture of which I had only listened to the prelude. I assured Jahns that on my arrival at Mallorytown, a village some four miles distant, I would send a doctor to properly dress Rue's wound. To this proposition he assented, but suggested that brandy would be very convenient for bathing the hand should inflammation set in. I promised him a bottle of the stimulant, knowing full well that the inflammation which he was anxious to allay, had not only set in but had long since become chronic. As I prepared to depart Rue gave a tug at my elbow and said, "Won't you look at my picter?" Then she ventured to ask her mother for the promised reward.

"I didn't get no picter," was the answer, "but I bought you a beautiful pair of shoes."

"Shoes," repeated Rue, with scorn on her lips and anger in her eyes.

Mrs. Jahns handed her the shoes. The moment they touched her hands she flung them into the fireplace, in which a great fire was burning, and then stalked out of the cabin without uttering a word.

Madam was so dumbfounded that she did not attempt to rescue them until they were as crisp and shrivelled and shrunken as her own soul.

Fearful of future consequences I placed a silver dollar in her hand, with which to purchase another pair. Bidding Jahns a cordial good-bye, I departed. As I trudged along to the ruins of the old mill my heart was filled with unutterable sadness for poor little Rue. What could I, a penniless lawyer, do for the child artist? For the first time in my life I prayed for wealth. Then came the wild resolve, I will steal the child and take her with me to New York. The thought of the attic office, the squalid surroundings, the dirty avenue and the children who played in the gutters, told me that the project was madness. Bad as was her lot here, it would be infinitely worse in the great city. There would be no great chestnut tree, no Chitter, no sparkling river, no whispering pines, no flowering golden rod, no voice of nature speaking to her, sympathetic soul in a language which only the children of genius can interpret. I sat down on a stone by the wayside and the hot tears coursed down my cheeks. There was a rush from behind, the swirl of a dress, two little arms clasped tight around my neck, two blue eyes looked up into mine filled with infinite pity and tenderness, but brave eyes scintilating with hope and comfort, and faith in the future.

"Don't cry 'cause your going away," she whispered, "you'll come back again, back again. Listen! hear the pines saying, 'back again, back again.' You hear them, I know you do. They'll tell me all about you when you're gone. Don't be afeared."

A far-away look stole over her face, as if she were gazing beyond, and beyond, away out into the great world and the future. She lay quite still in my arms, and then slowly closed her eyes as she murmured, "Some day I'm going away too; away over the great sea, and into such a beautiful land, full of castles and flowers and big, big towns, where there's an old, old city, older then Billa La Rue's tomb. Oh my!" she clasped her hands," the pretty picters, and the dear little angels, and the marble men and women and children, they can't talk to you, but they'll speak to me all day long and come and whisper in my ear when I'm fast asleep and tell me how to paint. Don't you wish you could see them? Some day, bimeby, we'll go and make them a visit, but we've got to come back here first and sit on Grandpa's big flat stone, and then the pines will tell us what to do. I know, but I won't tell; not now, anyway."

She kissed me first on one cheek and then on the other, saying, "Take them away with you." Then she sprang from my lap and in a minute she was gone.

When Rue had disappeared I walked rapidly forward. As the sun was setting behind a great blue mountain I entered Mallorytown, a little hamlet not deserving the name of village.

A hurried inquiry brought me to Dr. Lane's comfortable office. Explaining the nature of the wound and my desire that he should visit Rue the following morning, I paid his modest fee and departed for the hotel, where, after a substantial meal, I secured quarters for the night. Making inquiries for some old settler who was trustworthy, the landlord directed me to Squire Mallory. I found the Squire at his comfortable home. A glance at the man convinced me that he was the proper person to carry out the plan which I had formed. He was an elderly man yet full of vigor, acute in his intellectual faculties and, I soon discovered, possessed of a fund of humor, common sense and shrewdness rarely met with.

In brief terms I explained that I wished to make some inquiries relative to a family by the name of Jahns, which resided near La Rue's Mills. The Squire gave me the following facts:—The Jahns family was originally from Wales. They were all distinguished United Empire Loyalists and, down to the last descendant were Tory in politics, Church of England in religion and aristocrats in every fibre. The original founders of the family in Canada had received from the Crown vast estates in the district of Johnstown. They built the first mills, and for many years played an all important part in the political history of Upper Canada. They, with a few other leading families, had constituted "The Famly Compact," an alliance which had secured all the offices of honor and emolument in the infant colony. The Jahns had been lawyers, judges, high sheriffs, while, in recognition of his services, one had been knighted by the King. The advent of responsible government, to which they were bitterly opposed, brought about their

downfall, though at the present time several of the name
held positions of trust in the government service. By
gradual gradations their fortunes had declined. The
broad acres had been alienated, and to-day the survivors
were as poor as their ancestors had been rich. Fred-
erick Jahns, to whom my inquiry referred, had been
left an independent fortune. He had received a liberal
education and had travelled extensively in Europe.
Graduating as a barrister with distinguished honors he
had never entered upon the practice of his profession.
To supply his wants he had, at a very early date, replen-
ished his exchequer by selling off blocks of land. Acre
by acre his patrimony slipped away. Unfortunately at
the same time he acquired a passionate love for the
wine which sparkles in the cup. (The only thing which
he ever acquired, said the Squire with a merry twinkle
in his eye). To complete the catastrophe he married
an estimable lady, when only a few hundreds remained
at the credit side of his bank account and a few acres
of land in his possession at the mouth of La Rue's
creek. A little girl was born but the mother never
recovered. On her death-bed she induced Jahns to
transfer the land to the infant daughter. It was a wise
step as it has made a home for Jahns in his old age.
Left with an infant, he made the final plunge and in a
few months married the German woman who had been
secured as a nurse for the child. The step was a matri-
monial failure but a financial success. From the day
of the ceremony he has not had a moment's peace but he
has always had something to eat and a small supply of
brandy. Jahns never does any work, he relegates the
work and the talk to his German half. He pores over

musty books and lives in the past. Once a year he becomes the man of old. The day before Christmas he dresses himself in a faded suit, a relic of his departed prosperity, with knee breeches and silver-buckled shoes. Once donned, Jahns assumes the jaunty manner, the courtly grace, the punctillious politeness of the old colonial school. The transformation is marvellous. His intellectual activity revives; he is witty, humorous and satirical by turns; a charming companion; an ardent admirer of pretty women, and equally ready to discuss a glass of Burgundy or the latest social scandal.

During his holiday week he visits his relatives and old-time friends and companions. On New Year's Day he makes his calls and drinks his glass of wine with a grace which the youth of our time cannot hope to rival. The next day he disappears in his cabin, only to come forth smiling on the following Christmas.

"The little girl is a stepdaughter of the present wife," I remarked.

"Yes, fortunately for the peace of the world," answered the Squire.

"She goes by the name of Rue," I suggested.

"Yes, that is La Rue, writ short." I don't think that she was ever christened and the German gave her the name of the place where she had lived since her birth," answered the Squire.

"Be that as it may," I said, "I wish to place a modest sum in your hands annually, which is to be expended for her benefit."

The proposition met with Squire Mallory's hearty approval.

My instructions were that one hundred dollars per

annum (it was a third of my income) should be used as follows:—Two complete suits of strong, comfortable clothing, one for summer the other for winter. She must be sent to the district school six months in the year, even if resort had to be made to the arm of the law against Jahns. The balance of the fund to be expended in materials required for drawing and painting in oils and water colors. Rue's decision as to what she required to govern the selection made. No local teachers were to be employed, and the child was under no circumstances to be informed as to the source of her income. When she grew older, if she wished to write she was to do so through Squire Mallory.

I returned to the hotel well pleased with my arrangement, which looked to the welfare of the little artist. When I reviewed the occurrences of the past few days I could scarcely divest myself of the thought that it had all been a dream.

My solitary companion, with whom I struck up an acquaintance, proved to be a Member of the Canadian Parliament and a lawyer from the county town, Brockville. To him I explained the object of my search and after reviewing the circumstances decided to place the case, relative to the title, in his hands, as the Titles Office and the archives at Ottawa were open to him for inspection at all times. His knowledge of Canadian law, in such an undertaking, was also highly necessary in arriving at a correct conclusion. Mr. Woods informed me that at least three weeks must elapse before he could give me a decided answer, but as I was in Canada it would be best to remain, as a consultation might be necessary as the investigation proceeded.

In my boyhood I had been an ardent disciple of the gentle Isaac and now saw an opportunity to renew my acquaintance with the finny tribe.

My friend informed me that the sport was far superior in the inland lakes to that found in the St. Lawrence and that Charleston Lake would in every respect realize my sanguine expectations. The next morning, furnished with a letter of introduction to mine host, Armstrong, of Farmersville, a village some twelve miles distant, I set out on foot for my destination. My spirits had risen with a bound. The leafy arbors through which I passed, the fields golden with ripening grain, the bracing Canadian atmosphere, combined in supplying a tonic which braced my nerves and recalled the days of long ago, when I climbed the banks of Kauka Lake in dear old Yates County. At high noon I strode into Farmersville and presented my letter to the landlord. My welcome was cordial and in five minutes I was at home. From Armstrong I learned that the lake was some five miles distant and that he owned another hotel at that point to which I would be conveyed after dinner. I sallied forth and secured a supply of fishing tackle at a village store.

Evening was coming on as we drew rein at Cedar Park. Before me nestled a blue lake, stretching away and away into deep shadows and long bays, which faded by insensible degrees into cloudland and mist. Beyond, a single mountain peak, bathed with the last rays of the setting sun. Little islands nestled here and there; wild fowl sped by seeking a resting place for the night. It was early Canadian autumn in this north land. The atmosphere was a mellow, opal tint, such as one sees in old paintings. Here and there the first frost had touched the tips of the soft maple leaves, transmuting them into red and gold, where they hung in clusters amid their green companions. The row-boats, coming and going, left behind a wake of liquid silver burnished by the setting sun.

The inn fronted the west and, from its broad balcony I drank in the entire scene at a glance. Well had it been named Cedar Park. On every side grew the beautiful cedars, not in artificial regularity, but as the winds of heaven had scattered the seeds. Some in solitary exile, Cain-like, driven from the family; mostly in clusters and bunches with winding paths through which you could push your way. Every shrub and tree, the grass itself, was in a state of nature. Brown patches, where no grass grew beneath the deepest shade, gave forth the smell of "old mother earth." Beyond were, here and there, flickers of sunlight, which struggled through the branches, and still beyond, the open and undulating sward, broken by little hillocks with long tufts of grass giving the impression, at a distance, of miniature castles set in a plain.

I rubbed my hands with supreme satisfaction as I thought that this was to be my home for three long weeks.

The days which I spent at Charleston Lake will never be forgotten. The salmon which I hooked, coming to the surface from ten fathoms beneath, and cold as ice, the game black bass and the beautiful moonfish, with alternate scales of silver and black, (which I invariably put back into their native element, receiving, as my reward, the satisfaction which I felt in seeing them dart away) combined in producing unalloyed happiness.

One forenoon I had landed from a small bay upon a rocky island, and had thrown myself on the grass beneath a great pine. A tangle of alders grew on the margin and shut out a view of the lake, save a small opening through which the almost level rays of the sun glinted. I heard the splash of oars and, looking down, at my feet, saw an anchor heaved overboard from a boat. The solitary fisherman had decided to try his luck in the quiet little nook.

As I was not likely to be observed, I fell into a daydream from which I was suddenly aroused by a shout followed by "Ha! I have got you at last."

I peeped through the opening, and saw a very tall man, dressed in a black, threadbare frock coat, such as my grandfather had worn. The trousers were of the same material, only more shiney and polished; an enormous collar with ragged edges projected above his ears; a black stock encircled his neck with the bow under his right ear, while a pair of angular bony hands grasped an immense bamboo fishing rod. The strange fisherman had sprung to his feet, his battered silk hat was floating on its crown between the boat and the shore. The bamboo rod swayed to and fro. Then began a pantomine never excelled. The lank, long figure with a bald head and a few grey hairs blown hither and thither, the swaying boat, the bending rod, two great flashing eyes, a firm-set mouth, made up the component parts. As if spurred by an electric shock, this grotesque figure darted from stem to stern of the little craft and back again, falling repeatedly over the centre seat, oblivious to all save the fact that he had hooked a fish. His eyes blazed as he shouted.

"Aha! No you don't. I've got you," until, losing his balance, he fell backwards upon his back in the middle of the boat. This unexpected movement gave the rod a sudden upward jerk, and, much to my surprise, a perch, not weighing more than half a pound, dangled at the end of the line. I had expected a ten pound salmon. "This is glorious," exclaimed the prostrate fisherman, as the perch swung backwards and forwards over his head. Then he sat up, seized the fish with his left hand and pointed one bony finger of the right at the captive, muttering at the same time, "You cormorant, what have you done with all the minnows which you stole from my hook? Don't wink at me, you rascal. You are my enemy and I shall treat you as King Thackembau treated his enemies. I shall eat you."

Suddenly placing his hand on his head, he discovered that his hat was gone, but he soon recovered it by fishing it out on the end of his rod.

Raising the anchor, he paddled the boat to the shore, jumped out with an agility which was surprising for a man of his age. Breaking his way through the alders, he strode up the bank and we were face to face. I arose and said "Good morning." He did not even give a start of surprise, but, in a deep, sonorous voice said, tapping himself on the breast, "Ecce Homo," and, pointing to the perch, "Ecce Pisces." He next proceeded to clean the perch, kindled a fire, cut a forked branch upon which he impaled his enemy and began toasting him before the fire, a gleam of intense satisfaction wreathing his countenance. As if suddenly recalling my presence, he exclaimed, "Where is that perch now?"

"On a forked stick," I replied.

"True, corporeally," he muttered, "but where is he spiritually?" he continued, nodding his head.

"That's a metaphysical question of your own asking, which you must answer," was my reply.

"Just so; let me see, that perch was a great sinner. He wouldn't work. 'He toiled not, neither did he spin,' but waited for me to catch the minnows which he ate. I knew him of old. I telephoned to him down my line admonishing him to repent, but he actually winked at my warning. Then I chastised him. I hooked him repeatedly in the jaw, but always gave him a chance to get off and turn over a new fin. Time and again I have brought him to the top of the water. What a pitiful look he had in his eyes; contrition and repentance. I could see that he was crying, but the moment he was free he always gave me a leer with his left eye, which boded my minnows no good. He must have been a perch of excellent taste. What a beautiful quiet nook he lived in. When he wanted excitement he could swim out to the point where the big waves dash; a turn of his tail and he was in calm water again. Didn't his environment have something to do with the formation of his character? Who knows but what some low perch visited him at times and sapped his morals? Was he responsible for his acts? That is the question which has puzzled me for a long time."

"A similar question has puzzled a good many people," I remarked.

"I think he must have inherited a good many of his

traits," continued my visitor, "but I never knew any of his ancestors. I could forgive him for all that he inherited. The *must* should always be forgiven, the "ought," sometimes. Yet he actually cultivated those traits to the highest state of perfection. While I waded in the brook to catch minnows, I could hear him laugh though he was miles away. There were times when I actually admired the sly dog. I'd come here, put down my anchor and then wait, not putting out my hook. He was always watching, but would grow impatient, and finally rise to the surface and disport himself in the sunlight, flashing back gleams of gold on his sides. A stranger would have said, 'There's an innocent perch.' But I knew him. It's but temptation writ a new way. His home was under that great weed, which rises and falls with every pulsation of the lake. It faced the morning sun and got shelter from the mid-day heat by a branch of that great elm. But all this don't answer the question—where has he gone?"

"No," I said, smiling.

"I know where his corporeal part will go," continued my philosophic friend, smacking his lips. Then he brushed back his iron grey hair and said in a whisper, "Do you believe he is in perch heaven?"

"In perch heaven?"

"Yes, perch heaven."

"You said he was a great sinner."

"Yes, but how do you know that he didn't repent after I hooked him, and how did he know that it was wrong to steal my minnows, and was it wrong for him to steal them if he could not help it?"

"He has suffered death, anyway," I replied.

"Yes, and fire," said my strange companion, who produced from his coat pocket a large piece of bread, some raw onions and four hard-boiled eggs; inviting me to join in the repast, which I did, but carefully avoiding his enemy, the perch, which was done to a turn.

Then we drifted into a desultory conversation, during which I learned that my acquaintance was a physician, who had retired from active practice. He informed me that he was nearly eighty years of age, and that he ascribed the preservation of his wonderful vitality to the fact that for many years he had spent the greater part of each summer upon the waters and islands of this charming lake. In a spirit of mutual confidence I gave him a short account of my first case.

"There is but one solution which I can suggest," he remarked.

"What is it?" I inquired.

"Consult the witch."

"Consult the witch; what witch?" I asked.

"The Witch of Plum Hollow," he replied.

"Where does this modern Sibyl reside?"

"Only a few miles from here."

"Am I to understand that you believe in witches?" I asked with astonishment.

"I am an old man," he remarked. "The ignorant and the superstitious ascribe supernatural powers to certain persons, whom they designate witches. I am not ignorant and by nature the reverse of credulous, and yet I am not, by any means, prepared to say that by a purely natural law, which for want of knowledge we ascribe to the miraculous, persons do not exist who intuitively arrive at conclusions many degrees removed from the normal. It is also very extraordinary that when you investigate such phenomena you always run plump up against a woman. She may have been the Witch of Endor, a member of the Sisterhood of the Delphic Oracle of Greece, a vestal Virgin of Rome, or one of the Fox Sisters of Rochester. Any woman of average capacity possesses the intuitive power of arriving at a correct conclusion in a much higher degree than any man. She does not reason, she simply decides, and that is what you require in your case. Take my advice, young man, and consult the Witch of Plum Hollow, and use your own discretion in being guided by her advice."

"Surely Canada is yet wrapped in medieval gloom," I exclaimed.

"Don't forget that out of medieval gloom came the light," was the quick retort.

The following morning I secured the only horse in the village and rode slowly away over the hills in quest of the Witch of Plum Hollow. As I journeyed along I felt a profound contempt for myself. Here was I, a practical New York lawyer, striving to settle the knotty points of his first case by consulting a Canadian witch. Absurdity could reach no greater heights. As I inquired my way even the county yokels grinned at me derisively. In an hour I was in front of the small loghouse in which the modern Sibyl lived. It in no wise differed from similar habitations. I knocked timidly at the door, which was opened by a young woman whose complexion was a cross between that of a Gipsy and an African.

"Can I see the Witch of Plum Hollow," I inquired boldly.

An amused expression crept over her face as she asked, "Do you want your fortune told?"

"Yes," I answered.

She pointed to a ladder in the corner, by which ascent was made to the attic.

I mounted the ladder and found myself in a garret. The furniture consisted of a small pine table and two chairs. The witch, who was seated at the table, was a little old woman, who, at first, paid not the slightest attention to my presence. Her age was uncertain; probably seventy, if not more. A kindly expression lingered about her eyes and the trace of many smiles about her mobile mouth. "A kind-hearted old lady," was my mental conclusion, and at that moment I pronounced my friend, the doctor, a bit of a wag as well as a philosopher.

Finally the witch raised her eyes and gave me a look which I shall never forget to my dying day. She did not look at but through me. Probably it was imagination upon my part, but at that moment I felt that my very soul was being weighed, measured, probed, and analyzed. Noticing my embarrassment she said, in a low, soft voice, "Won't you take a seat?"

I complied, and at that moment the Gipsy-looking girl placed on the floor at my feet a small tea-pot, from which the steam was hissing, and two tea-cups. The witch motioned for me to place the pot on the table and then said, "Will you turn a cup?"

"What do you mean?" I asked.

She poured out a cup of tea, first shaking the pot

vigorously, and then carefully re-poured the tea into the pot, taking care to have the tea grounds in the bottom of the cup, which she inverted and twirled bottom up on the table.

Thus instructed I repeated the process and handed her the cup, at which she merely glanced, saying, "Turn another cup."

I complied. This cup she examined very carefully, and then, pointing her finger at a bunch of tea leaves, said, "Do you see that great flat stone with the bones of a dead man under it."

I had firmly resolved to betray not the slightest surprise at anything which she uttered, but in spite of my self-control I gave a start. Then I peeped into the cup and shook my head. There shot from her eyes a look which said, "Doubter, already you begin to tremble."

At her request I turned another cup. Ere she examined it I was startled by the great change which had taken place in the witch. It is best described as the consciousness of power. The hesitancy and indecision of extreme old age had given place to energy and purpose. The hand which took the cup no longer trembled. The tint of health was back in her faded cheeks, her eyes blazed and scintilated with an all-consuming fire, which froze the very marrow of my bones. At that moment something told me that the witch saw nothing in the cup itself. She was probing, fathoming my inner consciousness. Her first words were, "You are seeking that which you shall not find, but will find that which you seek not."

Then she paused as if noteing the effect of her message.

"At the flat stone you met your destiny, there you may find your happiness. You must go back to that spot and take the path leading into the hills. If you are a laggard you will abandon it, if a coward desert it. Therein lies your fate. Mark the cabalistic seven. If you wander in strange lands do not despair. The desert sighs and moans for water. Death will clutch you by the throat. But you have done a kind act and God never lets a kind act die. If you could but read that which is writ on the great flat stone? Well may you say that you are blind."

As she proceeded I closed my eyes. Imagine my surprise when upon opening them I saw before me the old woman who had met me when I entered the attic. The same smile lingered about her puckered mouth and ran in little ripples out upon her withered cheeks.

She chatted in a pleasant way about the weather and when I asked her the amount of her charge said simply, "only twenty-five cents."

With a hearty shake of the hand I bade her good bye. I found that my pony had slipped his bridle, and I did not see him again until I sighted Cedar Park, where he awaited my return and graciously accompanied me to his stable.

As I was pushing my boat from the shore the next morning the philosophical doctor made his appearance on the little pier. He too was prepared for a day's outing, as he carried his great bamboo rod in his hand, while from the fit of his coat I concluded that his pockets were plentifully supplied with boiled eggs. I invited him to accompany me for the day. He clambered in and I pulled away. The morning mists were yet lying in the little bays, but rapidly rising in the open lake, where the sun's rays tinted the crests of the little waves.

The doctor sat in the stern enjoying the panorama of islands and water with a background of Laurentian grey rocks dotted with sentinel pines. Blue Mountain towering into cloudland, with the rising mists sweeping across its ragged face completed the picture.

"The Indians," said the doctor, "have a very pretty legend which accounts for all these islands. It is that a long, long time ago the Great Spirit, in passing over the lake, held in his hand a bunch of flowers which he dropped. As they descended the wind caught and scattered them. Where each flower fell an island sprang up. That islet, pointing to a mere dot a few feet in diameter, came up where a stray blossom fell."

"That is an Indian poem," I remarked.

"Yes, but we call the first comers savages, while at the same time paying the highest honors to the few white men who imitate the savages. Why not honor the Indian poets as well as our own?"

Then he raised his eyes to mine and asked, "Did you go to see the witch?"

"Yes."

"What do you think of her?"

"I think her a very remarkable woman."

"Then she surprised you?"

"Unquestionably."

"She has even surprised me," he continued, when I thought that my day for surprises was over."

"Have you any theory by which you account for her wonderful powers?" I queried.

"Certainly, certainly, I always have a theory for everything. Theories have always been my hobby, practice never." Then with a half-pathetic look at his threadbare coat, "Theory has made me as poor as a rat, but why should a man of eighty care, who possesses six boiled eggs, half a loaf of bread and an excellent digestion? He can laugh at fortune." Then his hearty laugh rippled across the waters and died away in reverberations amongst the overhanging cliffs. When the last echoes had gone I said, "What is your theory about the witch?"

"You have no doubt read of the monks of the east," the doctor replied, "who spent their lives in solitary contemplation in the desert; of Budda and his followers, who gave themselves up to communion with nature and their own thoughts; of the medicine men of this continent and of the islands of the South Pacific; of the fakirs of India and the dervishes of the Soudan; of the Himylaian Brotherhood and the disciples of modern Theosophy. These men by isolation and contemplation acquire in a remote degree the powers which nature has bestowed upon the Witch of Plum Hollow. Humanity grows and buds, and finally blossoms. It may be but once in a century; time is but a small factor in intellectual development. Who can tell how many eons were necessary to produce a Shakespeare and a Goethe. The witch represents another type, equally wonderful and equally potent for good; did we but comprehend her place in the economy of the universe. For I am by no means certain that her powers are confined to this little world. The Witch of Plum Hollow is the antithesis of the mathematician. Where humanity is deaf, she hears; where the million are blind, she sees. You ask me why? How? I cannot tell. She belongs, as yet, to the unknown, but by no means the unknowable."

"May I hazard the opinion that she is a mind-reader?" I interjected.

"My young friend," he exclaimed, "what is a mind-reader?"

"I mean that she is not able to seize upon any fact which is extraneous to the mind of her subject. Beyond that point she simply gives rein to her imagination."

"That is, she may tell you that of which you are cognizant, but possesses no knowledge of the future."

"Precisely," I answere

"A beautiful theory," he exclaimed, "beautiful—but lame in the left leg, and blind in the right eye. Yes, a beautiful crippled dwarf. Did it ever strike you that a man's brain is a photograph gallery, where all the images and impressions are registered as negatives are preserved. The greater the number of convolutions of the brain, the greater the capacity of the gallery. Now if you admit that the witch can look into that gallery of negatives and examine its contents, it is only a simple question of deduction for her to *predict* what results will follow. If you grant the first power, the second follows as a logical sequence."

"But," I interjected, "what she sees she knows, the future she only guesses at."

"A point well taken," replied the doctor. "The

astronomer only sees a limited part of the orbit of a comet. Yet he predicts its re-appearance to a second of time. In the deduction rests the test of the powers of the witch, of her intimate knowledge of human nature; fully as accurate as is that of the mathematician and ranging over a wider sphere. In its highest development prescience is known to us as the miraculous. To me it signifies pure reason, and is no more a miracle than is the growth of a blade of grass; that is, it is in consonance with natural law."

"That is to say, the witch knows what I will do better than I know myself."

"Certainly," was the reply, "she is a witch, while you are only a lawyer." Then he suddenly cried out, "While my head has been in the clouds I have been sitting on the eggs."

I burst into a hearty laugh, while the doctor raised the skirts of his coat and spread them out like a fan on the sides of the boat.

The remainder of the day was spent in pleasant converse, and that night my conclusion was, that the Canadian doctor was one of the most delightful companions it had been my lot to meet. A letter from Brockville, calling me to a consultation with Mr. Wood, terminated my visit to Charleston Lake.

Mr. Wood's investigations had elicited no new facts. Billa La Rue's property had fallen to the only heir, his wife, by whom it had been sold previous to her death, with the exception of a few acres. Of my client, not a trace had been discovered. The most thorough inquiry amongst the old settlers demonstrated that he had never been seen in that part of the country.

Thus baffled, but in nowise disappointed, for I had grown into the belief that I should never see my strange client again, I determined to return to New York. My preparations were soon completed, when the thought came upon me that in so doing I should neglect the advice of the witch, who had admonished me to search the ravine which led into the hills. I had not the slightest faith in the undertaking, but my duty to my client said, "It is the last chance, exhaust it and be at rest."

Finally I decided to devote a single day to the search. Noon the next day found me seated on the great slab covering the remains of Billa La Rue. I brushed away the moss which had grown over the inscription and read :—

Here Lies the Body of
BILLA LA RUE

Born at Bath, England, Aug. 7th, 1727.

Died at his home, Upper Canada, Aug. 7th, 1817.

The thought that there was a peculiar coincidence in the birth and death came suddenly upon me with great force. He died in the same month, and on the same day of the month on which he was born. Then there flashed through my mind the remark of the witch, "Mark the cabalistic seven." The cabalistic figures confronted me. Born and died on the seventh day of the month, and in years also ending in seven. Then I recalled the fact, it was the 7th day of August when my strange client called upon me in New York. Of course, this was only a coincidence I argued, but such had been the nature of my recent experience, that I was half inclined to attach undue importance to the discovery.

The day was a delightful one; soft and balmy. The leaves on the great chestnut rustled and murmured, while Chitter disported himself in its branches, no doubt impatiently awaiting the arrival of little Rue.

I looked down the winding path which ran away zig-zag between the hills and lost itself among the hazel bushes.

With a sigh of resignation I set out upon my search. The absurdity of the act came upon me with redoubled force. Here was Carl Martyne, a New York lawyer, plunging into a tangle of brush and bramble, in a Canadian forest, seeking he knew not what, merely to gratify the whim of a garrulous old woman, whom an eccentric doctor had been pleased to call a witch.

Absurdity could reach no greater bounds, that was my sole consolation. I would soon be in my office and shake off all such morbid fancies.

I buttoned up my coat, tucked up my trousers, and set out with a firm step and at a good pace, determined to spend the remainder of the day in the bush.

For an hour I trudged forward, following the path which ran alternately east and west, save when it crossed a hill to gain the next valley. Thus wandering back and forth I knew that in a straight line I had not advanced more than half a mile from my starting point. The path was fairly well beaten, having been trodden by cattle which roamed through the glades in search of the succulent grasses growing on every side. Gradually the way became more rocky, the hazel bushes thicker, and the character of the country gloomy and desolate. The sloping and verdant hills gave place to precipitous cliffs, on which grew a stunted juniper covered with spines.

I no longer saw marks of human footsteps. Little springs gushed out from the hillsides, at which I assuaged my thirst. I kept my eyes well about me for any signs of a former visit by man, but discovered nothing which indicated his presence, save here and there the stumps of pines which had been cut probably half a century. The nature of the undergrowth proved that at sometime in the past the land had been cleared by lumbermen of all the great trees. In a short time I lost all reckoning of my position. I knew that I was gradually working my way to the north, by the zig-zag process, but how far I had advanced I could not conjecture.

Fatigued with my exertions, I sat down upon a grassy hillock and fell into a contemplative mood. Feeling drowsy I reclined upon the elastic sward and fell asleep.

How long I slept I know not. When I awoke the sun had disappeared behind the ridges and the air in the valley had grown damp and chilly. I was very hungry. Glancing at the sky I made a mental calculation as to the point due south. A happy thought suggested itself, I would make a short cut across the ridges, and pass the night with my friend, the old lady who had emptied my flask.

There was no time for delay. I set off rapidly, climbing one hill and almost sliding down into the next valley. My speed was tremendous, and I congratulated myself upon the fact that half an hour would bring me to the river. Fast the shadows of night fell; the approaching night only accelerating my speed. I plunged through brake and bramble, fell over tangled vines, and finally completely out of breath and exhausted, paused and looked around me. The surroundings were inexpressibly lonely and dreary. The ground was strewn with huge boulders. I was bathed with perspiration. The moment I recovered my breath I poured forth a volume of expletives, all of which referred to the Witch of Plum Hollow. Then I actually burst into a loud laugh over my egregious folly in chasing a Will-o'-wisp through the Canadian forest. The cold night air, for it was now pitch dark, warned me that I must be up and moving. I groped forward slowly, animated by the vain hope that by chance I might stumble upon the path, and thus find my way out. Not a star was visible. While pushing through some bushes, I suddenly felt the earth give way beneath my feet. The next instant I plunged into space and landed on my back in a tangled grape-vine. I had probably fallen twenty feet, but owing to the bushes and brambles checking my descent, I was only scratched and not seriously injured. The accident convinced me that it would be dangerous to attempt to proceed. I must pass the night where I was. Mechanically I began to search my pockets, and was rewarded by finding a solitary cigar. The match with which to light it could not be found. I had abandoned hope—when I discovered a solitary lucifer. Then with infinite care and great caution I searched about on my hands and knees for material with which to kindle a fire. I gathered small twigs and dry leaves, with some cones from the pines, and heaped them against a great log which lay prostrate on the ground. The task was full of excitement. Then I removed my coat and spread it carefully over the heap, so as to furnish a shelter from the wind. With trembling hands I struck the match.

No miser ever clutched gold with greater love and tenderness than I bestowed upon that lucifer. The flame flickered uncertainly for a moment, then caught in a piece of birch bark and burst forth in a ruddy glow. I gave a cheer which rang out on the night air and came back in mocking echoes. For an hour I was kept busy gathering fallen branches and securing boughs with which I built a camp to shelter me from the wind. The pines on the hill moaned and sighed. Having arranged things to my satisfaction, I sat down and lit my cigar, which I smoked with the supreme satisfaction known only to the bushman. For the first time I experienced to the full the consolation which lurks in the fragrant weed. Rising to replenish the fire I threw on some branches, and in so doing, knocked the cigar into the fire. In an instant I clutched the ends of the burning sticks and hurled the fire from the back-log into which it had burned. While thus engaged, my eye fell upon a metallic substance in the centre of the great log, which proved to be hollow. I reached down and brought forth a small iron box, which had thus become exposed to view. It was so hot at one end that it burned my fingers. Wonder of wonders. I could have sworn that it was the identical box which my client had left with me in New York. So implicit was my belief that I drew the key from my pocket, inserted it in the lock, and opened the box. When open I caught sight of a piece of paper which was smoking, in fact, one end was burned black and fell in cinders when I picked it up. The remainder was so badly scorched that I deposited it between the leaves of my pocket memorandum book, lest it too should fall into pieces. In the bottom of the box I discovered two curious pieces of stone. It was undoubtedly owing to their presence that the paper had not been completely destroyed by the heat, as it must have rested upon them. These stones I carefully examined. One was a pyramid of polished quartz about an inch in diameter at the base and running to a fine point at the apex. The other was a green stone, such as I had never seen, but which I have since learned is found in New Zealand, and is extensively used by the Maoris of that country in making charms and ornaments. This stone was circular, its diameter being the same as an English sovereign, but it was considerably thicker. On one side was a small hole or indentation, which penetrated only half way through the piece. The reverse surface was exquisitely polished, upon which were cut in intaglio a kangaroo and a large bird, which I mistook for an ostrich. I have reason since for believing it was an emu. A savage, who held in his hand a crescent-shaped stick, was depicted standing beneath a cross formed by stars. At his feet rested an arrow with the head pointing toward the outer edge of the disk. The green stone, when rubbed on the sleeve of my coat, gave forth lustrous sparkles. Were these stones merely playthings, the whim of some savage, from whom they had been taken, or did they represent a purpose? I placed the crystal pyramid on my knee and put the disk on the top of it, trying to balance it there, but did not succeed.

Removing the green stone, I mechanically polished it on my coat and again placed it on the crystal apex. The result startled me; it not only remained in position, but oscillated with that motion peculiar to the magnetic needle. I concluded that I had solved the mystery, it was simply a stone compass. When I looked at the direction in which the arrow pointed, and at the north polar star, which was visible, I made the discovery that this unique compass did not point to the north, but very nearly east. After a great number of experiments, for the green stone had to be rubbed each time to excite the magnetic properties which it contained, I finally decided that the mysterious stone was equally liable to point in any direction. It was evident that I had not discovered the use for which it had been intended. I abandoned the problem in disgust. Placing the curiosity in my pocket I drew forth the half-burned paper and attempted to read its contents, but, as it was crisp and fragile, I concluded to defer the examination until under more favorable circumstances.

Morning dawned at last. I made a hurried search for my hat, but failed to find it, took a survey of the position of the sun and set out once more. I had not proceeded half a mile when I came upon the path by which I had entered the wood. In a few minutes I found myself again under the spreading branches of the great chestnut tree, from whence I hurried forward to a fisherman's cottage on the bank of the river. As I approached the man met me on the beach and immediately burst into a loud guffaw.

"Can I get some breakfast and secure you to row me to Gananoque?" I asked.

"They gave you a hot run for it this time," was his answer.

"Who?" I inquired.

"Who?" he repeated. "You know who." The peelers. Uncle Sam's peelers," and then he chuckled with evident satisfaction.

"I have been lost in the woods all night," I said in an impressive tone.

"Oh, yes! I understand," winking at me. "You've been lost, but you didn't lose the 'pop,'" pointing at the same time to the iron box. "You're a pretty sight, now ain't you. You wasn't scared—oh, no. How you must have run. But how did you get across the river?"

"I tell you that I have not been over the river."

"Oh, no! none of you chaps go *over* the river; you live and die at home. Just coming back from camp-meeting with the collections in the box. Been on a mission to the heathens," and again he laughed until his sides shook.

"What do you mean?" I asked, half angry with the fellow.

He paid not the slightest attention to my question, but continued, "Where are your chums? Gone to Washington, I guess, to interview Jim Blaine on the Chinese question. You've lost your hat. You're a pretty sight—your own mother wouldn't know you." Then sinking his voice to confidential whisper, "Don't be skeered. You're in Canada, where you'd better stay."

I looked at him in utter amazement.

"Come in out of the cold," he exclaimed, "you've had it hot enough."

I went into the cabin for I was nearly famished.

"Nance," he exclaimed, "look at this critter. He's an orfan, looking for his Ma in the woods."

Nance laughed.

"Tek a chur, tek a chur. You lost babe, crying in the wilderness. I say, hes you got a pipe?"

"No."

"Any terbacker?"

"No."

"Any money?"

"Yes."

"I thought so; you fellows always have the chink."

"Who do you take me for?" I inquired.

"What do you take me for?" he answered. "I know you. I know the whole gang. You hung on to the poppies."

A faint light dawned upon me. I was mistaken for a member of a band engaged in smuggling opium into the United States.

"My friend," I remarked, "you are mistaken about me, I am a lawyer."

"That's good," he exclaimed. "A lawyer is just the man to get away. Slippery as a greased eel and tarnation sharp. I know now why you got away."

Seeing the futility of further discussion, I abandoned the controversy, and hailed with delight the announcement, "Breakfast is ready."

The meal over, I borrowed a slouch hat, stepped into the boat which the fisherman had ready, and in a few hours was in Gananoque. His last words, when bidding me good-bye, were, "Hang on to the poppies."

Thus ended my first visit to Canada. The next day found me in my office in New York. My first act was to arrange with my banker so that the annuity for little Rue should be paid quarterly to Squire Mallory.

Then I set to work to examine the burnt paper found in the iron box. I pasted it carefully on a strong sheet of paper so that not a fragment would be lost.

Below is a *fac simile* of the document:—

West

under

* *
* * in lat. 4
* *
tude 129. G. E.

deposit of rich

guarded by the

life if discovered sacred

Oasis 30 miles amid

approached

the hills to the three falls

greenstone at midnight

arrow when it dips

red gumtree due South

and then at right angles

then running tunnel

to black o o o o o o o o

Put in fire

B. L. R.

For hours I pondered over this chaos of words. At first I could make nothing out of it. Then I took to consulting maps and gazeteers, with but little better success. Lat. 4 might signify any point from forty to forty-nine, or it might mean simply four. The "tude" before 129 was the termination of longitude, but I had no means of deciding whether it was east or west. The word "Oasis" suggested that I must first locate a desert, and, in consequence, I very carefully scanned the great African

Continent, but arrived at no solution of the mystery. The stars, I finally decided, must refer to the Southern Cross. This directed my attention to South America, Australia and the other great islands in the South Pacific. Day after day I returned to the task, only to abandon it in disgust. The word "greenstone" gave me a weary search over the map of New Zealand, for I had ascertained that such a stone was found in those islands, but at the same time I made the discovery that it was also obtained in large quantities in the interior of China. The figure on the disc, which I supposed represented an ostrich sent me back to Africa. In fact for months I oscillated from one continent to another and then to the islands of the sea. By insensible degrees this burned piece of paper bred in me a desire to visit these far-off lands. The desire grew into a passion. I could not sleep. The books of law became repugnant. The spirit of unrest was upon me and could not be shaken off. The ambition to become a leader at the New York bar disappeared, and in its stead reigned an impulse to wander too and fro on the face of the earth. I had no well-defined plans, and yet I could not divest myself of the impression that in some way I was destined to solve the mystery which lay hidden in that bit of charred paper. When six months had elapsed, with no sign from Billa La Rue, and, as I had not secured a second client, I resolved to abandon the practice of my profession in New York and make a bold stroke for fortune in a foreign land. I decided upon Australia. I sold my scanty library and arranged with the janitor of the building to send my first client to the Bank of Montreal, should he call, where I left a cheque in his favor for the balance remaining out of the sale of the gold, after deducting $300 for my expenses and services. I departed for San Francisco, secured my passage on the Oceanic liner "Mariposa" for Sydney, N.S.W., where, after an uneventful voyage, I landed. A hasty examination of the geographical features of the great island, coupled with the word "west" at the head of the burnt manuscript, influenced me in selecting Western Australia as the basis of my first investigations. From a teacher of navigation I took a limited number of lessons, which enabled me to calculate the latitude and longitude of a place. I then purchased a quadrant and the necessary instruments required in making observations, secured my passage on a coast steamer sailing for Freemantle, a port near Perth, capital of the colony to which I was bound. On my arrival at Perth I ascertained that an expedition, which was destined for the interior, was in course of formation. News had been received that two prospectors had struck a payable alluvial gold field, and were rapidly amassing fortunes. No time was to be lost by those who were anxious to be first at the new rush. I offered to become one of the party, and much to my delight the offer was accepted. The captain being influenced in his decision to admit a new chum in consequence of my being a lawyer, as my professional services would be valuable should any dispute over claims arise. The remainder of the party of twenty was made up of experienced miners and bushmen. When I had bought a horse and my share of the outfit, my slender resources were exhausted—only a five-pound note remaining. The exact locality of the new fields was not known, so that, to a great extent, it was a leap in the dark. A strip of desert country intervened between the most advanced sheep farm and the coveted country, but this did not deter us from plunging boldly into the Australian bush. For two weeks we traversed a sparsely settled district, inhabited by a few squatters, and then entered upon the sand plains. Here our progress was extremely slow, owing to the scarcity of water and the absence of vegetation for the horses. Most of the travelling was by night to avoid the intense heat. There were days when we must have perished for the want of water had it not been for the acumen displayed by one member of the party, who guided us to the precious fluid in the most unlikely places. This man's prescience in this department almost reached the supernatural. The water-finder, which was the name applied to him by universal consent, was Jess Hibbard. He was an Englishman, about fifty-five years of age, of sturdy build, black hair, a low, broad forehead, and an expression about his eyes which is best described as sullen. A heavy, square chin denoted great resolution of character. I had observed from the start that Hibbard was not a favorite with the remainder of the party, but after a time, in consequence of his services, this feeling had gradually worn off. We all recognized our indebtedness to him, and yet there was an indefinable something which prevented good fellowship. This treatment was not in the least resented by the man, but rather accepted as a matter of course. As a new chum I was never consulted by the leaders, but I gradually drifted into an intimacy with Hibbard, from whom I learned many secrets by which he was able to ascertain the presence of water beneath the surface of the drifting sands. One night we camped in a little valley, in which the grass grew with a luxuriance which was fully appreciated by our half-starved horses. After the camp fire had been lit, I noticed that Hibbard was wandering about carefully examining the ground. A smile of satisfaction, which I had never seen before, wreathing his lips. In the morning not a horse was in sight. I started down the ravine thinking that they must have strayed away more than the usual distance. My heart leaped into my mouth as I came suddenly upon my own hack, stretched upon his side in a little hollow and stone dead. I saw that he must have died in great agony, as the ground was torn up for yards around. The cold sweat came out on my forehead as I pictured myself compelled to complete the journey on foot. I started to return and inform my companions of my misfortunes, when I stumbled upon another dead horse. Fully alarmed I hurried to the camp and spread the evil tidings. Every man sprang to his feet. A hurried search was made, and in half an hour we knew that all our horses were dead. The explanation was very simple, they had eaten of a poisonous weed. This weed is well known in Western Australia and has in many localities prevented the settlement of the country, as it is equally fatal to all kinds of stock. At the spot where we camped none was visible, but at a little distance, where I had noticed Hibbard wandering about, it grew in great profusion. A hurried consultation was called and the question of further advance debated. The majority were in favor of establishing a depot at the spot where we were, in which most of the supplies could be deposited, and then returning to Perth for new horses and additional provisions. For my part, I knew that a return would mean my abandoning the enterprise, as my funds were exhausted. A few, in a half-hearted way, proposed a forward movement on foot, but this idea was scouted. Hibbard, when appealed to, gave his opinion freely. He would not advise any man to go forward, though he believed that a few days advance would find us in the kangaroo country, where a plentiful supply of meat could be secured. For his part, he could subsist on a meat diet; he had done so before; he had long since made his choice. He would go on, even if compelled to advance alone. If so, he would mark his trail, so that it could be followed. Should he discover the field, he would locate a large claim on the best part, and hold it against all comers until the arrival of the expedition. If he perished, that ended the matter, so far as he was concerned. The laconic way in which he gave his decision convinced me that I had not misjudged the man. There was a dogged tenacity of purpose which would confront any danger standing in the way of his success. By noon it was decided that the members of the party should return to Perth, leaving Hibbard in charge of the depot. Should Jess decide to go forward he could leave a note to that effect. A cache was built, in which the mining equipment and the provisions were deposited. At the last moment I made my decision and said, "I will stay with Hibbard."

"No! no!" was the universal exclamation. "You are a new chum, and where Hibbard would grow fat you would die like a dog."

This imputation of weakness on my part roused my combativeness and confirmed me in my decision. Having elected to become his companion, I turned to him for some mark of approval. Not a sign of encouragement or dissent was manifested. He went on smoking his pipe with the nonchalance of a savage.

"What do you say, Hibbard?" I asked.

"Right you are, new chum," was the answer.

"Shall I pull through?"

"Pull through or die," came forth amid wreaths of smoke from his pipe.

My companions renewed their expostulations. The captain then called me to one side and said, "See here, Martyne, I want to tell you a thing or two, and I don't want your death charged up against me. Jerry Hibbard is a lag."

"A lag," I repeated. "What is a lag?"

The captain burst into a loud laugh over my ignorance.

"A lag is a convict, and in this colony a convict is a ticket-of-leave man. Jerry can go where he pleases in Western Australia, but he cannot leave the colony; he is a lifer. He can't get out by a ship, the police stop that; he can't get out by land, the desert stops that. It is a clear case of stop, you see. What his character is I don't know, but one thing I will tell you," and he whispered in my ear, "If Jerry Hibbard finds himself face to face with death from starvation he will kill and eat you."

I shuddered and shook my head.

"It won't be the first time," continued the captain, "that the likes of him have eaten comrades, and won't be the last. Now you know the truth, you can go or stay, as you wish,"

PLUM HOLLOW.   67

I did not credit the indictment, and answered boldly, "I will stay."

Ten minutes after Jerry and I were alone.

After the departure of the cavalcade, his first remark was, "The captain told you I was a lag."

"Yes."

"You might have known it by my walk, but you are a new chum."

"How?"

"See here," he said, thrusting out one foot. "Look at that."

The ankle, which was exposed, must have been heavily ironed for many years. So long that the skin had grown down and over the manacle, which, when removed, had left a great band, over which the skin yet hung, never having regained its original position. Hibbard smiled grimly as he gazed at this evidence of his past life, and then burst out with a vehemence, which, to me, was a new phase in his character.

"I'm going to get out of this accursed country. With plenty of gold I can bribe a ship captain at Freemantle. Without gold I shall cross the desert and make my way to South Australia, or die in the attempt. And then for home—home, home."

His voice mellowed and broke. The word recalled memories of the dim past, when he was an English boy in his native village, wandering amid the green hedges, when his father read the evening prayer and his mother kissed him good-night; when he played truant from the parish school. Then he was full of truth and innocence and hope. Now, a great rough ticket-of-leave man, full of passionate hatred and oaths, and, for aught I knew, a soul seared with some great crime.

"Never mind, old fellow," I said, "we will pull together, and if the time ever comes when I can help you to escape, say the word."

He answered not, but said, pointing to the small case slung at my side, which contained my sextant, the greenstone disc, and the crystal pyramid, together with a nautical almanac and the scorched paper, "I have often wondered what you carry there."

I explained to him the nature of the contents, not mentioning the articles found in the iron box.

"Such things are of no use in this country," he remarked, "where the sun shines by day and the southern cross points the way by night."

We decided to remain at the depot for several days and recuperate ere we set out on our long march. During this time we made a careful selection of the articles which we considered absolutely necessary. They included a billy (a small tin pail), a pannikin (a tin cup), a blanket, a small quantity of flour, tea, salt, with a gun for each and a plentiful supply of ammunition. The outfit, with the exception of the gun, was rolled up in two blankets and when carefully tied constituted our "swags." We had everything ready for a start the next morning. Before going to sleep Hibbard warned me of the dangers which lay before us and declared that he would be well pleased should I remain at the depot until the arrival of the party from Perth.

I declined to consider the proposition. In a few minutes we were sound asleep. It seemed but half-an-hour when I suddenly awoke and sprang to my feet. The night had waned, and the east was purple with fast approaching day. The camp fire had burned low, a mist hung over the little valley. Hibbard was lying with his feet almost touching the ashes, his blanket twisted about his breast and his head supported by a root of the eucalyptus under which we camped. Intently I listened. There only smote my ear the rustle and flapping of the bark on the great white gum trees as it swayed to and fro. Grim spectres were these shadowy strips guarding the secrets of the interior of a vast island continent. Half asleep I sought my blanket again. The next moment I was wide awake. Suddenly, as if by magic, a hundred naked savages emerged from the gloom. They were silent as the grave, but stood around in three circles, each man of the inner circle held poised in the air a bamboo spear, while those in the outer circles grasped a nully nully as if about to strike. I closed my eyes, my heart stood still, not a sound broke the awful stillness, which spoke of eternity. Hibbard turned uneasily as if conscious of impending danger, then without warning sprang to his feet. There was a fierce yell, a struggle, a blow which sent a thousand stars spinning before my eyes, then absolute darkness. When I recovered consciousness I was lying on the same spot, a dull and heavy pain in my head told me that I had been struck a frightful blow. How long I had been lying there I could not tell, but the sun was high in the heavens. Hibbard was coolly dressing a wound in the calf of his right leg, through which a spear had been thrust, while the blood slowly trickled from a frightful gash over his left eye. In not elegant English he was cursing all niggers from Africa to Van Dieman's

Land. Noticing that I had regained my senses, he said, "Little Yank, we are in for it."

"What will become of us," I asked.

"They will probably cook me for supper," he replied, "but you'll escape; too thin until you fatten up."

The leer on his face, which mingled with the blood coursing down his cheek, gave me such a horror that I relapsed into silence.

The ground was strewn with broken guns and revolvers, from which it was evident that the natives knew the nature of firearms yet were too ignorant to use them. No guard so far as I could discover had been placed over us. I was too weak to think of making my escape. After Hibbard succeeded in staunching the flow of blood, he turned to me and said, "New Chum, if I were you I would cut and run for it, now is your chance, while they are dividing the plunder."

I shook my head. "No I will not leave you."

He gave a start of surprise and then said, "There is more game in a Yankee than I ever dreamed of, but all the same if I were in your shoes I'd run."

"No," I said doggedly, "I shall stay until you are able to go with me.

What our fate was to be I could not guess. I only knew that many of the tribes in the interior were cannibals. "Perhaps we are going into the Leichardt business old fellow," remarked my companion.

"Who is Leichardt," I inquired.

"Only a white man that the niggers caught and have held a captive for thirty years," was the reply.

I noticed that a consultation was in progress between a few who appeared to be vested with some

PLUM HOLLOW. 71

authority. Then they came and motioned to us to get up. I arose at once but Hibbard simply pointed to his wounded leg. They paused irresolute for some time and a savage raised his spear and pointed it at the wounded man, who did not flinch but eyed the fiend with a coolness which I have never seen equalled. After considerable delay they produced two poles and placed them under Hibbard's arms, two stout natives standing at the end of each pole. By this means the "water finder" was raised to his feet and half carried along, for we at once set out for the east. Our progress was exceedingly slow, as every five minutes there was a revolt among the pole-bearers, who had to be changed before we could go forward. We camped ere the sun went down, and as they had plundered the cache of all that it contained, we were thrown some hard tack and a fragment of an opossum, several of which had been killed during the day. Tired out and exhausted we soon fell asleep. In this manner we proceeded for five days, when we halted at a spot where the remains of old camp-fires proved that the tribe had recently made its headquarters. Being reduced to a diet of meat, for all of the other supplies were exhausted, I was upon the verge of starvation, finding it almost impossible to eat the half-cooked meat without salt. Hibbard, as the captain had predicted, grew strong and hearty and rapidly recovered from his wounds. What surprised me was that the case which hung at my side and which contained the sextant had not excited the cupidity of our captors. No doubt they attached some mysterious meaning to the box, the import of which I did not know.

On mentioning the subject to Hibbard, he suggested

that I should take out the sextant and gaze intently at the sun, the object being to impress the savages with my importance. I tried the experiment, and immediately found myself surrounded by the entire camp. Much to my disappointment each one wished to look through the instrument. An old chief came forward and attempted to wrest it from me, but I resisted, fearing that it would be broken. In trying to replace it hurriedly in the case the green disk rolled out at my feet. In the twinkling of an eye a great change came over the faces of the entire throng. Awe and fear struggled for supremacy. They fell back to a respectful distance, bowed their heads and muttered prayers or incantations. From that hour my position was fully established. I was treated with the respect and consideration due to a medicine man or a rain-god, but my exact rank I was never able to ascertain. After a few days spent at the central camp, the natives divided into small parties, composed of a few families, each party taking a different direction. Hibbard and I were retained by an old chief who possessed considerable authority. Our course lay over sandy ridges, which were barren of vegetation, a scanty supply of water being found in the deeper valleys. After several weeks wandering we entered upon a bush country, in which kangaroo, the native bear, opossum and emus were fairly plentiful. Much to my delight we came upon great quantities of nardoo seed, which Hibbard and I gathered, crushed between stones, and from the flour baked damper, which, being a change from a meat diet, I greatly relished. Frequently we discussed the probability of making our way to the coast, should we escape, but

PLUM HOLLOW. 73

Hibbard declared that our only hope lay in waiting until the tribe wandered into the vicinity of a squatter's station, which was certain to come to pass if we had patience. Some nine months had elapsed since we had been taken captive, and yet the course of our travel tended toward the interior. One evening we came to a halt in the centre of a great valley. The stream, which in the flood, must have been a very considerable river, was now dry, save pools which remained at distances of from ten to twenty miles. The heat was so intense that parrots and cockatoos frequently dropped from the trees, only to be seized and eaten by the natives.

Hibbard and I were engaged in making crude moccasins for ourselves from a kangaroo skin, which we had partially tanned with a decoction of wattle bark. Our clothing had long since disappeared. We were girt about the loins with a wallaby skin, and carried with us a rude attempt at coat making, formed by sewing together opossum skins. The coat was only used as a covering at night and during the rainy season. Our feet were torn and blistered, and caused us intense pain. The country had been gradually changing for some time. Away to the north and east loomed the dim outline of a mountain range, the birth-place of the stream at our feet. For several months I had cultivated the good-will of a young native, who had shown an aptitude for acquiring a knowledge of the English language. Jagga Jagga had now a smattering of pigeon English, which at times was very amusing. It was a wonderful combination of vowels, gutterals and expletives with pantomime accompaniments. Jagga Jagga stood by, watching our attempt at shoemaking, at the same time expressing his contempt for such useless articles. To emphasize this contempt he thrust his toes into the shingly pebbles in the dry bed of the stream, and rapidly dug with his iron toes a hole fully a foot in depth. His foot was equivalent to an iron rake, and apparently equally lacking in sensibility. Hibbard reached over and picked from the debris a small irregular-shaped stone, which was water-worn and coated with a green slime. Not a muscle of his face betrayed excitement, and yet I felt that he had made an important discovery. He carelessly dropped the stone under a piece of the kangaroo skin and proceeded with his work.

When Jagga Jagga went away, my companion said in a whisper, "Look here." Taking up the stone, he rubbed it, and there came out from beneath the slime a dull yellow gleam, which, once seen, can never be mistaken. In Hibbard's eyes gleamed a phosphoritic fire, luminous in intensity. Greed and exultation married in a look. The find, to this man, meant not only riches but liberty. As he gazed upon the nugget, in his soul he heard music infinitely sweeter than the clank of the irons when they fell from his ankles. A minute since he was a captive, now a *free* man, and at home in "Merry Old England." I could distinctly hear the beating of his heart. The one thing which he coveted was within his grasp. Then he grew deadly pale, his hands trembled, but the next instant the blood surged into his face, dyeing it crimson. "Ah!" he panted, "at last, at last—mine, mine, mine."

Recovering from his excitement, he carefully hid the nugget, which must have weighed twenty ounces. Then we strolled away, to discuss the situation.

"My mind is made up," said Hibbard.

"What do you purpose doing?" I asked.

"Bolt the first chance. Come back here and dig."

"How will you subsist?"

"Just as I do now."

"How are you going to cross the desert, provided you find plenty of gold?"

"Give me the gold first, the desert will keep."

"Can we make our way to Freemantle?"

"When I get my swag I'll make my way to England."

"How far are we from the coast?"

"Probably a thousand miles."

"When will you leave the savages?"

"In about four days."

"Why so long a time?"

"Because we may be followed, and at the same time we must not lose sight of the trail which will lead us back. Of course you will come, he said, eyeing me in a curious way.

"Yes, I will venture it."

From that hour we carefully laid our plans. As we went forward Hibbard and I broke many branches from the trees, overturned stones, marked the sand with rude arrows pointing in the direction from whence we came. On the fourth night we carefully noted where the best bows, arrows and spears were thrown down, as well as the remnants of the supper and a small lot of nardoo seed. The night was clear and bright. Above blazed the constellations of the south. Such was the intensity of the light that we could see distinctly for miles. If pursued, this meant danger, on the other hand it would prevent our losing the trail. He who has not wandered in Australian solitudes can form no conception of the ease with which one is lost. A sameness characterizes bush and plain, whose monotonous regularity confuses and bewilders all but the most experienced bushmen. The Eucalypti, the Shee Oak and the Ti-Ti tree, the scanty brown grass growing in patches, the gullies with yellow corrugated sides, worn by the winter rains and baked by the summer heat, the wattle bushes by the streams, and the mallee thickets cover the country for countless leagues.

Long before midnight, for your savage sleeps soundest in his first nap, we stole away. Once free from the camp our progress was a steady trot. We reeled off mile after mile. The thought that we should be hunted and perhaps killed, gave wings to my feet. I knew that if pursued Hibbard would abandon me to my fate and go on alone, without a qualm of conscience.

There were times when I thought that I heard the cries of the enraged blacks and their footbeats on the sand. We paused not in our flight until morning dawned. Then we waded into a slough left in the bottom land, climbed from the water into the branches of an overhanging tree, and from branch to branch and tree to tree worked our way directly above a fern tree gully, into which we dropped, and from which spot Hibbard ordered me not to stir, on the peril of my life. Hibbard thoroughly understood the extraordinary intelligence displayed by the black trackers and had taken every precaution to guard against it. All that day we lay concealed, not daring to light a fire. In the early evening we ventured forth and continued our journey. Daylight, the next morning, found us in close proximity to where the nugget had been discovered. We made a detour of a few miles, and determined to spend a few days in hiding, so as to give the blacks plenty of time to abandon the pursuit.

On the fifth day we advanced to the river bottom, and found ourselves on the spot where Jagga Jagga had raked out the precious metal with his toes. Above the sun glowed like a great ball of fire. On the shingly beach were scattered flakes of mica, irregular fragments of quartz and grey slate, highly polished in their journey from the distant mountains, washed down in the spring flood.

Not being provided with any semblance of mining tools we fell to work with our hands, picking up the larger stones one by one and carefully examining, lest we should throw away a nugget. Hour after hour we toiled. My hands were soon lacerated and the nails worn down to the quick. Scarcely a word had been spoken. The light of hope and expectancy died out in my breast, despondency and gloom clutched me and mocked at my calamity.

"Pshaw," I exclaimed, throwing myself on the ground and giving way to bitter reflections. "With the natives it was bad enough, but here we may starve, and not another ounce of gold will ever be found."

Hibbard paid not the slightest attention to my lamentations.

"You would plunge boldly into the infernal regions for gold," I muttered, and then the warning words of the captain, "He would kill and eat you," flashed into my mind.

Not a word came from Hibbard's lips, his low forehead was contracted, the lines about his mouth sharp set. He toiled on alone for hours, until his patience and perseverance won my admiration and commanded my respect. As night was coming on, I attempted to kindle a fire by rubbing the pointed end of one stick in the groove of another, as I had seen the natives do. I labored with great energy for half an hour, but was compelled to give up from sheer exhaustion. Then Hibbard seized the sticks, and in five minutes had a fire, his only remark being, "You Yankees are good for a dash, but if you want a bulldog, get an Englishman."

"Did you find any gold?" I asked, anxious to turn the conversation into another channel.

"Not a grain," he answered.

"What are we going to do next?"

"Dig."

"With our hands?"

"No."

"How?"

"I will show you."

We cooked the last of our supplies for supper, and woke up the next morning face to face with starvation.

"Martyne," said Hibbard, "you must hunt while I dig. If you get the opossum I will get the gold."

I provided myself with a nully nully and a spear, set out on my search for game, and late in the afternoon killed a young opossum.

On my return to camp I found that Hibbard had not touched the mine, but had spent the day in fashioning a shovel by means of the fire, for we did not even possess a knife. He had secured a branch which the wind had blown down, which was fully eight inches in diameter. This he slowly burned off at the required length. Then he reduced it in size, save about a foot at one end, by turning it constantly in the fire, and at the same time moving it lengthwise. Great care had to be exercised, lest the fire burned in too deep, but by constantly scraping off the cinders with the edge of a piece of slate, he finally succeeded in reducing the handle to a diameter of about two inches. This left the stick in the shape of a great maul. To form the blade of the shovel he heated stones in the fire to a red heat, then pulled them out with sticks, and so arranged the stones that they gradually burned the end into a flat surface, which became thinner and thinner at each application of a hot stone. With round boulders he formed the concave part of the blade of the shovel. It was a great, heavy, clumsy thing, of no practical use, when it received its last baptism of fire. During the two following days, while I was away hunting, Hibbard succeeded, by first scraping with the edge of slate stones and then rubbing with sand, held in a piece of kangaroo skin, in reducing and polishing his shovel into a handy utensil, well fitted for the purpose for which it was to be used. When the handle had been oiled with some opossum fat, it shone with an excellent polish. The shovel completed, Hibbard set to work on the mine.

He cleared a circular spot, about thirty feet in diameter, of the large stones, and then began throwing out the small pebbles and shale. I soon noticed, as the work progressed day after day (for I had become by this time better acquainted with the haunts and habits of the opossum, and now kept our larder well supplied), that the stones appeared to have been deposited in our mine in concentric rings, the larger ones on the outer circumference, and growing gradually smaller as they approached the centre, where only minute pebbles and some sand were found.

"Surely," said I, "at some time the natives have built these rings of stone in the bed of the river."

Hibbard laughed. "Whoever heard of a native building anything?" he exclaimed.

"Who put them there then?" I inquired.

"The current of the river. Don't you see that this has been a great eddy at one time, and therein lies our hope."

Day after day Hibbard toiled on, I giving some assistance. Not even the color was found. It was shale, and quartz, and mica followed by mica, quartz, and shale. Foot by foot the digging slowly sank. Day by day the sun mounted higher in the heavens, for Christmas was fast drawing near. After a month's toil, one evening the shovel, now half worn away, punctured the last of the gravel and revealed a stratum of reddish brown clay, beneath which lay only a few inches another stratum of white clay.

"That ends the mine; a dead failure," I said to Hibbard, who had ceased work.

Great beads of perspiration gathered on his forehead and rolled down his cheeks. He carefully scraped up a shovel full of the brown earth, climbed out of the shaft and proceeded to the water hole, some ten rods distant. We did not possess even a cup. So he placed a handful of the earth on a flat stone and dipped up a handful of water, which he let trickle through his fingers upon the earth beneath. Repeating this process again, the little heap began to swell up, then spread out, disintegrated and gradually ran away in tiny yellowish red streams. With bated breath I watched the experiment until I saw a gleam of yellow metal. Hibbard caught sight of it at the same instant. It was nearly round, very smooth, and the size of a small bean. Then were revealed other pieces, from the size of a shot to that of a pea, but not a trace of fine gold was discovered, the current had carried it further down the stream.

We laid the dull yellow pieces on a eucalyptus leaf and gazed upon them with the fond admiration which a lover bestows upon his mistress. There we sat, the ticket-of-leave man and the New York lawyer animated by the same passion, worshipping the same yellow god. The following day we secured a log, about six feet in length and two feet in diameter, which had been burnt off from a fallen tree. This log we set on its end in the ground on the margin of the water hole, so that it projected above the ground about two feet. Then we heated round stones, and gradually burned out a cavity nearly equal to the diameter and fully eighteen inches in depth. A strong pole, and a dipper made from an opossum skin, completed our outfit. On the shovel I carried over the brown clay, which contained the pay dirt, and dumped it into the barrel, as we termed the burned-out log. Hibbard kept the barrel filled with water, and vigorously stirred the contents with the pole, constantly replenishing the water which was washed over the top, carrying away the earth and sand held in solution, and allowing the gold and small quartz pebbles to sink to the bottom.

At night we washed up, by taking out the contents of the barrel and re-washing it in the dipper. By a crude balance, which Hibbard constructed, we divided the gold into equal shares, which we carefully buried in pouches made from the skin taken from the tails of kangaroos. In two weeks we exhausted the claim. We burrowed under the walls and fossicked in the bed of the stream in many places, but failed to find any payable place. It was evident that Jagga Jagga had hit upon the rich deposit. As nearly as we could judge we had obtained nearly one hundred pounds by weight of the precious metal. We were anxious to make our departure, fearing the return of some of the natives. I pointed out to Hibbard that with such a load to carry our progress must be exceedingly slow, and that our best course would be to travel directly west. This course must bring us eventually to the coast, but in all probability we should come upon some outlying sheep station long ere we reached the sea. In any event he could count on my assistance in escaping from the colony. I had concluded to abandon all search for a solution of the La Rue mystery, and return on the first ship to my native land. The long leagues of desert, through which we had passed with the natives, was the obstacle which stood between us and civilization. Hibbard explained that we were entering upon the attempt at the worst possible season of the year, and, in conclusion, related the story of Burk and Wills. To remain, Hibbard believed, would be to be taken captive again by some wandering tribe. Thus confronted by dangers, we decided to proceed only by night stages, as the Australian savage rarely ventures from his camp after the sun goes down. We went forward by easy stages until the character of the country warned us that we were approaching the confines of the desert. There we halted and secured a supply of meat, which we smoked and dried, thus reducing it to the least possible space and weight, and, heavily laden, set forward on our march. The gum trees gradually disappeared, the vegetation grew more sparse and stunted, animal life nearly vanished. At every point of the compass stretched a plain of undulating sand. At great intervals we came upon the beds of streams run dry, and there, after digging about two feet with our hands, we generally succeeded in obtaining a scanty supply of brackish water. A few kangaroo rats, which we killed, furnished us with food, but to sustain life we were compelled to encroach upon our dried meat, but husbanded it with the greatest care, feeling that the time would come when our preservation would depend upon it. For days the wind had blown constantly from the north, increasing the heat, which became frightful in its intensity. I could only compare it to the hot air from a blast furnace. A marked change was gradually taking place in our mental faculties. We lost, to a great extent, the power of speech. We saw, on the distant sands, beautiful lakes, flowing streams and nodding groves of fern trees, all of which danced and shifted, and finally disappeared as we drew nearer, only to re-appear again on the verge of the horizon. Our progress could not have exceeded ten miles per day. One morning when we staggered to our feet the sun was no longer visible, only a red blur in the sky marked its position.

"We must find a shelter," Hibbard articulated with

difficulty, pausing between the words, as if he had forgotten his mother tongue.

"Why?" I inquired.

"Buster—a buster is coming on," was his answer.

We stumbled forward and in half an hour found ourselves at the foot of a little hill, the broken sides of which faced the south. A vast bank of sand lay on the crest of the hill and great winding heaps beyond to the south, leaving a little valley or gorge which must have been thirty feet in depth. Into this gorge we rolled, down the yielding bank. Up and in under the face of the rock were a number of vertical openings, into one of which we crawled for a few feet, and there lay completely exhausted. From our refuge we caught glimpses of the open desert beyond. The air was full of shifting, driving sand, worn to an impalpable powder by the friction of the particles one against the other. For minutes one could not see a distance of ten feet, though we were, to a great extent, sheltered from the fury of the storm. The stifling heat, the intense thirst, for we had not a drop of water, the swirling dust, which penetrated to every part of our bodies, all conspired to check perspiration. I felt that a pent-up volcano was raging within me, vainly attempting to find an outlet. My ears and nostrils were full of dust. My eyes pained with an intensity which I had never before experienced. My tongue protruded from my mouth, hanging out on my swollen lips like a piece of leather. As I tossed from side to side, I noticed that Hibbard had buried his face between his hands and was lying prone upon his stomach. He never moaned or attempted to speak, and for aught that I knew was dead. The wind shrieked and whistled and sighed and moaned with a fiendish fury which nearly sent me mad. Suddenly a new sensation came upon me; the sensation that my head had swollen to an immense size, that my eyeballs were bursting from their sockets. My head grew larger and larger, it filled the shelving rock whereon I lay, bulged out into the ravine, rolled over the great sandy plain and finally filled all space, blotting out sun, moon and stars. Then I lost consciousness. How long I remained in a state of coma I never knew. My next sensation was that of inexpressible physical pleasure, not of active but passive bliss, of happiness born of rest. The war of the elements no longer concerned me; I was in a realm where care and anxiety were unknown. The past as well as the future were swallowed up in the present. It was enough that I suffered no pain, experienced no anxiety. I had lost the will as well as the power for motion, and in that knowledge was supreme content.

For hours I remained in this trance. Then suddenly there shot through every fibre of my being the most excruciating pain. With a cry of agony I sprang to my feet. What I experienced for a few brief seconds no pen can write. From Elysium I was at a bound plunged into the accumulated horrors of the infernal regions. Every nerve and muscle of my body was filled with a torment, which by degrees spent itself, leaving me weak and trembling. The storm had ceased, the sun was shining in the east, for it was morning, but the morning of what day I could not tell. The sand had drifted up nearly to the spot whereon I had been lying. A few hours more of the storm and I should have been buried fathoms deep beneath its winding sheet. Then came the sudden thought, where is Hibbard? Echo alone answered where. Not a trace of my companion remained. He had vanished. With energy born of despair I plunged into the little space at my feet, climbed to the apex of the sand hill, and strained my eyes in every direction. The storm must have been unique in its fury and intensity, for it had completely changed the appearance of the country. For miles and miles the monotonous level of the past had been succeeded by great hills and valleys inexpressibly beautiful in contour. Here rest great billows of spotless white, frozen in their tumult into waves of sand. Even the curl at the tips of the crests of the waves were there, speaking in mute tongues of the storm. Red and brown belts ran for miles in parallel lines through the great white ocean, which glittered with millions of quartz prisms.

In this wilderness of solitude and desolation I was alone. I carefully scanned the sand hill, seeking in vain for Hibbard's footsteps. Then I went back to the little cleft beneath the face of the hill. Half-buried in the sand lay the case which contained the sextant and the greenstone. Mechanically I opened it, why, I know not. The sextant was broken into a dozen fragments. I felt that it was intact when I entered that shelter, now it was useless. In my delirium had I taken it out and destroyed it and then replaced the fragments? I could not tell. The gold! I searched the spot whereon I had thrown it. It too was missing. Had Hibbard played me false, broken the sextant, robbed me of my share of the treasure and left me to my fate. I could not reconcile myself to such a conclusion. He may have gone mad, and in his delirium carried away my gold as well as his own and wandered forth into the desert, where he perished. He might have rolled from the shelving rock into the pit below, carrying the gold with him, and at this moment lie buried five fathoms deep. My bundle of dried meat was intact, and, as it was priceless in such a situation, I finally concluded that my suspicions were groundless and that in some way my companion had perished. I could not hope to solve the mystery. A raging thirst now possessed me and I immediately set out in quest of water; that I would succeed in finding any was exceedingly problematical. With no well-defined course in my mind I wandered for hours over the desert, but in vain. The sun was sinking in the west when I sat down on a hillock of sand and gave myself up to despair. I had been wandering in great circles, a fact of which I was cognizant, and yet powerless to prevent. I had read of many such cases and looked upon it as the precursor of my fate, which meant death in the desert. My spirit for escape from the toils was strong, but physically I was as weak as a child. Hope had died out and in its stead had come a stoic resignation to my fate. Why contend any longer with conditions which could not be changed? My mind wandered constantly to the shores of Kauka Lake, where my childhood days had been spent. I laved and splashed in its blue waters. I was at Cedar Park once again, with the crystal waters rippling in sweetest music on the beach. A spring gushed forth at my very feet. I was conscious, and yet unconscious. I knew that all which was passing like a panorama before me was but the creation of imagination, and yet, strive as I might, I could not banish the visions.

Thus forsaken and lost I arose and looked over the plain. Away out on the desert I saw a black speck. Surely it had not been there when I sat down. Was it a tangible object or the figment of a dream? I could not decide. With strength born of despair I set out in the direction of my discovery. As I advanced the impression on my mind was that the object itself was coming toward me. Doubt gave place to a certainty. It was a native, who carried in his hand a poised spear. I sat down and calmly awaited my fate. Death might come; for me all his terrors had fled. The savage came forward with that peculiar cat-like movement seen in its fullest perfection when the Australian native approaches his prey. It is not a run, not a walk, but an undulating, serpentine motion, full of boldness and caution, doubt and determination, whose end is DEATH.

Powerless of speech, I bowed my head and closed my eyes. A cry rang out, and the next instant Jagga Jagga stood before me. He was evidently wild with delight. He capered on the sand, to the right and then to the left, and in his anxiety to speak the broken English, which I had taught him, burst forth in a jargon, not a word of which did I understand. I could only point to my mouth. He comprehended in an instant, and led me tenderly away for about half a mile, where, in the sand, which he hurriedly dug up with his hands, a few drops of water slowly trickled in. These I lapped up with my tongue. I had to wait for half an hour ere another supply collected. This was fortunate for me, for I verily believe that had there been an unlimited quantity I should have died on the spot, such was the intensity of my thirst. My strength gradually returned, and as Jagga Jagga had in some degree recovered from the excitement, consequent upon my discovery, I finally succeeded in ascertaining that on the first day of the storm (for it had raged for three days) he had followed a flock of emus into the desert (the camp was on the confines of the plain), where he had been caught in the whirlwind of sand. Not so fortunate as Hibbard and myself, he had found no place of shelter, but during that time had been blown across the desert, or soon buried in the sand when he lay down. No white man could have survived the terrible ordeal without food or water, but this child of Australia came through somewhat emaciated, but free from any serious injury. His first quest had been for water, his next, for kangaroo rats, two of which he had secured when he caught sight of me. While telling me the story he had devoured one of the rats, in a raw state, with great gusto, and eyed the other in a way that indicated a desire to dispatch it also. I motioned to him to do so, but he pointed to my mouth, as much as saying, "That rat is for you." Then I showed him my supply of dried meat, and in five minutes after the second rat had followed its mate.

We camped for the night beside the water-hole, and in the morning I inquired where the native camp lay. Jagga Jagga swept his hand around an arc of ninety degrees to the east and shook his head. It was quite evident that he too was lost, but that fact did not, in the slightest degree, depress his spirits. He was so pleased over finding me that being lost ceased to give him any concern. His confidence in his ability to escape renewed in my bosom the spirit of hope. I urged him to make a start, but this he refused to do. He had found a colony of rats, and would not go until he had secured the last member of the family. With unerring instinct he led the way to the spot, though it was fully a mile distant, and by noon we had six rats in our possession. Returning to the water-hole he tore the skin from the rat's head with his teeth and then stripped it carefully from the rest of the body, taking care when he came to the feet not to pull it entirely off, but instead, he gnawed off the leg from the inside, leaving the foot attached to the skin. By this means he secured six bags, formed of the skins, which were absolutely water-tight. These we carefully filled with water, tied the mouths of the bags firmly with a piece of string which I found in my case. I threw away the fragments of the sextant, placed the carcasses of the rats in the case. Jagga Jagga tied the six bags of water on his spear, then we set out for the south-east; that being the point finally selected by the captain of the expedition. Our first day's journey led over the undulating plain, and was without incident. Late in the afternoon Jagga Jagga succeeded in finding water, where we camped for the night. As we possessed no means of kindling a fire, my companion was compelled to devour one of the rats without cooking. The next morning we refilled the rat skins with water and proceeded on our way. No persuasion upon my part would induce the native to travel by night. He believed that the darkness was filled with evil spirits. When the sun went down he crept close to my side and there remained until morning. In his fidelity and devotion I had unlimited confidence. The second day we entered upon the mouth of a great valley, with lowering black walls of sand on either side. It must have been thirty miles wide at the entrance, but gradually narrowed to from five to eight miles as we advanced. The place was strangely sublime in its desolation. We soon came upon water, which was of a peculiar green color. When I stooped down to drink, Jagga Jagga seized me by the hair and suddenly brought me to my feet. At the same time, by pantomime, giving me to understand that in a few minutes I would be dead. As we advanced, the hills, which enclosed the valley, gradually increased in height, and, outlined against the blue sky, made a picture complete in its desolation. From the foothills ran out great irregular patches of alkaline earth, which glistened in the sun, and at times looked like molten silver. To the west there gradually arose an impracticable barrier of barren rock. The valley constantly dipped as we proceeded, and from Jagga Jagga I gathered, in an imperfect way, that this was a good sign and at the end we would find an abundance of water.

During this day we saw no signs of animal or vegetable life. For this reason I named the place the Valley of Death. Perhaps we constituted the first funeral procession, I thought, as we trudged along. Down the valley blew a hot wind like the breath of a volcano. At times in its course it picked up the blistering sands and sent them scattering in scurrying clouds through the canyon. In many places the earth was puffed up from beneath, forming a treacherous shell, which gave way when trodden upon, and precipitated one from two to three feet upon a sub-strata of needle-shaped pinnacles, which cut the flesh like knives and inflicted painful wounds. In some places the wind had thrown the sand into mounds several hundred feet in height and miles in length. The third day through this frightful valley found us completely exhausted. We had only used two skins of water, and lay down at night abject objects of misery. I had expected that the rats would turn putrid, but owing to the extraordinary dryness of the atmosphere, the reverse was the case, they had simply shrivelled up and turned into mummy rats, which tried the teeth of Jagga Jagga. In the centre of the valley were no signs of vegetable life, but on the outskirts some coarse grass and a plant resembling sage brush now and again made their appearance. On the third day out Jagga Jagga caught two marsupial mice, each of which only made a mouthful for him. In no part did we find a drop of water which we could drink. I think that it must have been strongly impregnated with arsenic, the presence of that poison no doubt accounting for its intensely green color. At noon the fourth day the last drop of water was gone. From the date of the storm I had suffered severe pain in my eyes, caused no doubt by the injury inflicted by the minute quartz crystals being driven with great velocity against the ball of the eye. The inflammation was constantly increased by the great heat of the desert. I found myself falling over little hillocks of sand, and unable to see Jagga Jagga when but a few feet distant, and ere sundown I became blind. Yes, blind in the midst of an Australian desert; blind with no man near but an

Australian savage; blind and without water; blind and wandering I knew not where. Not until the blindness came upon me did I abandon hope. I sat down and would have wept, but even that relief was not given to me. My eyes were like balls of fire. Jagga Jagga raised the lids and no doubt peeped into the sightless pupils, then he placed one end of his spear in my hand, took the other end and led the way. Hour after we marched over the blistering sands. I knew that night must have fallen. I lagged behind with leaden footsteps. He pulled me along for a weary mile or two, and finally I fell an inert mass on the sand. Jagga Jagga came to me and gave me the last remaining bit of dried meat, but so swollen was my tongue and intense my thirst that I could not eat it. In a short time I fell into a state of stupor, half slumber, half delirium. When I awoke the stillness struck my soul with horror. I groped about me, and at first thought that the darkness was so intense that I could not see; then the fact that I was blind and in the desert flashed upon me. I called aloud for Jagga Jagga, there was no response. I had been left to die. The spear had been planted upright in the sand close by my side, and the piece of meat left at my hand. The hours crept slowly by, the sun came up. I felt its heat beating upon me. Face to face with death in its most cruel form, I mentally counted the hours when I must become mad from thirst and wander for a brief space over the desert, and then miserably perish. I heard a rustling movement on the sand and the next moment a rat skin full of delicious water was thrust into my hands. I drank until Jagga Jagga wrested the precious fluid from me. The faithful fellow had stolen away in the night, and, as I subsequently learned, he had travelled fully twenty miles, and returned with that which alone could preserve my life and give me strength to escape from the horrors which encompassed me. After bathing my eyes with a care and tenderness which I shall never forget, we set out again, and after a march which lasted the entire day, we came upon our haven of rest. I could not see, yet I felt again the velvety carpet of grass beneath my feet, the soughing of branches above my head, the touch of tender leaves which brushed against my face, the cry of the laughing jackass and the perfume of the flowering wattle. Each of which whispered and laughed and danced in my heart, so full was it with thankfulness and joy. Jagga Jagga led me to the bank of a running stream, which sang a refrain of welcome, welcome, welcome. The trials and dangers of the past, even my blindness, was forgotten in the transport of my joy. I drank the gurgling water, laved my burning eyes, and swung my feet in the little pool below. In a short time I heard the crackling of a fire which my faithful companion had kindled, then there floated on the air the aroma of meat cooking. I call it aroma, to me it was all that is entrancing to the sense of smell. The meal of roast opossum which I ate that evening beneath a blue gum tree will ever remain, with me, the acme of culinary art. Jagga Jagga built a rude shelter, which he covered with fern leaves, under which I rested. In half an hour I fell into a delicious slumber, from which I did not awake until called to breakfast the next morning.

On the second day I could see a little, and at the end of the week the inflammation had subsided.

I gazed about me in astonishment. We were camped in a great fern tree gully, the first which I had ever seen. As far as the eye could see the fern trees covered not only the valley, but also the sides of the ravine. The trees were from two to forty feet in height and many of the fronds were eighteen feet in length. Above towered gigantic eucalypti, some of which shot four hundred feet into the blue arch above. In an open glade, beyond the mouth of the ravine, stood half a dozen trees covered with flamingo-colored blossoms, a gorgeous mass of scarlet, which, in contrast with the intense green of the ferns, completed a picture only to be seen on this great island of the South Pacific. On the bank of the stream, which gurgled down the gully, there clustered bunches of the silver wattle, with great masses of yellow blossoms. Here and there, in the open, a few wild flowers disported themselves in the sunshine. The gem of these flowers Jagga Jagga called "War-a-tah."

After my recovery I wandered over the plantation, which, I ascertained, was an oasis planted in the plain, just beyond the end of the Valley of Death, traversed under such frightful difficulties.

The oasis consisted of a range of hills some twelve miles in length and of an average breadth of two miles. In the hills were a number of springs, which fed the streams running through the ravines. Game was plentiful, and Jagga Jagga soon discovered a species of fern, the roots of which, when roasted in the ashes, furnished an excellent substitute for potatoes. The fern roots, with a plentiful supply of meat, placed our culinary department in a state of efficiency superior to anything I had experienced since my capture by the natives. My companion settled down in this Australian paradise perfectly contented and happy, expressing not the slightest desire to seek the tribe to which he belonged. His fidelity and devotion had completely won my heart. He spent the day in securing food, and in making a gigantic bow and arrow and several boomerangs. After my many months of wandering it was an inexpressible relief to lie beneath the great fern trees and listen to the mocking cries of the strangest of Australian birds—the laughing jackass.

On one of our trips to the extremity of the oasis we came upon a clump of native cherry trees, well laden with fruit. To my intense surprise I discovered that the pits of these cherries were attached to the outside of the fruit. Some three weeks had elapsed from the date of our arrival, when one day I listlessly opened my case and took from it a few pieces of brass, all that remained of the sextant, the greenstone and quartz pyramid, and a copy of the burned paper found in the iron box. I gazed with a smile of contempt upon the cause which had led me into my present position. I did not regret the change which it had wrought in my life, though at that moment I had not the faintest glimmer as to the means by which I should escape from the oasis and reach civilization. There had been born within me a new spirit; a spirit of freedom which the Arab feels when wandering over his native desert. The thought of a stuffy New York office, even with clients and fees was intolerable to me in my frame of mind.

Here was I, Carl Martyne, sovereign undisputed of a princely domain, with an army of one black man at my command, ready to confront any invader. While thus musing I glanced carelessly at the transcript of the burned paper, found that eventful night in the Canadian forest and under such mysterious circumstances. My eye fell upon the word "Oasis." In a second my mental faculties were in full play.

It was possible that I was upon the very spot referred to in the parchment. "Absurdity could go to no greater lengths," reason cried out. By what means could any sane person account for the presence of Billa La Rue upon this oasis one hundred years ago. Fifty years past the great colony of Victoria was but a straggling settlement. South Australia and Western Australia belonged to the unknown, save a few isolated spots on the coast, touched by adventurous navigators. Imagination said, "Is it any more wonderful that Billa La Rue should have been here than that Carl Martyne is here?"

I took out the quartz pyramid and placed it upright on a flat stone (as I had frequently done before, while wandering with the blacks); I balanced, upon the apex, the greenstone disc, which vibrated for a moment and then became nearly still, but for a slight movement like the flutter of a bird's wing. I saw that the arrow-head pointed south, in the direction of the lower end of the oasis, where the country was broken by hills, indicating intense volcanic action. I removed the disc and again placed it in position. Greatly to my surprise the arrow pointed in the same direction as in the first instance. Was this a coincidence? No. Repeated experiments proved that for some unknown cause this unique magnetic needle now responded to an attraction which was a constant factor. Excited and full of vague hopes I called Jagga Jagga and pointed to the mysterious greenstone. He was thoroughly frightened, and muttered rapidly, in his own language, incantations to the spirits which he worshipped or feared. He absolutely refused to touch the uncanny stone, and motioned for me to bury it, digging, for that purpose, with his spear, a hole in the ground. When I refused, he contemplated me, with great pity lurking in his eyes. I gave him to understand that he must follow me, when he prostrated himself and moaned and wept in the most abject and heart-broken manner.

I picked the magnet up and started down the ravine, determined to carefully search the oasis to its most southern extremity. Much to my surprise Jagga Jagga followed, but at a respectful distance. To my command, to go back, he paid not the slightest attention. It was evident that he regarded my experiment as fraught with great danger, but, at the same time, he was equally firm in his determination to guard me from harm. The way led through a part of the oasis which I had not visited before. Our advance was along the banks of the little stream which shot through a narrow gorge, about half a mile from the camp, and disappeared amid a tangled mass of foliage, through which I forced my way with the greatest difficulty. I frequently consulted the magnet, and found that the general direction indicated did not vary. Our progress was so slow that when night came upon us we had not advanced more than two miles, but, as I was upon the point of abandon ing the quest, a re-persual of the paper, in which the word "midnight" appeared, convinced me that I should push on, as the moon and stars furnished light sufficient to discern the direction in which the arrow pointed. Jagga Jagga I sent back to the camp for the sticks, with which we kindled a fire, so that in case the sky should become overcast, we could proceed with our investigations. In half an hour he returned, but trembling in every limb, though he absolutely refused to abandon the search, the object of which I felt he comprehended, although I could not elicit any explanation from him.

As we carefully made our way through the shrubbery the spirits of doubt and fear contended for mastery in my breast. Doubt lest we were not upon a trail which would solve the mystery, and fear lest, if the trail were genuine, I should not be able to follow it, so defective were the materials in my possession.

The stream suddenly came to an end by rushing over a precipice and disappearing in the darkness below, into which I peered in vain. To more carefully examine the locality, I had Jagga Jagga kindle a fire, but this only served to show that we were in a dangerous place. The earth was rent by great fissures and covered with loose boulders, which, at the slightest touch, rolled down the hillside and fell with a splash into the water, some fifty feet below. By the aid of a torch we carefully explored the locality, and made the discovery that two additional streams also discharged their waters into the same fissure, thus creating three waterfalls within a few feet of each other. In the manuscript I read, "*the hills to the three falls.*" It might be simply a coincidence, but that was highly improbable. The fever of investigation coursed through my veins. I felt that the secret was nearly within my grasp. Could I solve it, or was I to be baffled at the last moment? In searching about the chasm I found that the rock lay in ledges, like a gigantic staircase, and the impression upon my mind was that, ages since, this descent had been improved by man; but this was merely a supposition, as the action of the atmosphere and the water had obliterated all conclusive evidence. With the aid of Jagga Jagga I constructed six small torches, and determined upon making the descent, which was extremely perilous, owing to the rocks being excessively slippery. By the light of the torch we groped our way to the bottom, which I estimated was from fifty to sixty feet from the surface. The three streams united in a seething cauldron of inky blackness, and then the water burst its way out through a rocky barrier.

The arrow on the greenstone still said "Follow the stream." This we did by clambering along the ledge and, in some instances, wading in the bed of the stream itself. When we had proceeded some distance we found our way barred by the trunk of an immense gum tree, which had blocked the passage. It must, from its position, have, at one time, grown in a cleft of the rocks in the defile, in which we were travelling. In diameter it was not less than twelve feet, and, as the bark had been worn completely away by the action of the water when in flood tide, the sides remained as slippery as glass. Here we halted, baffled and disheartened. Again I glanced at the parchment and read:—

"Red gum tree due south."

"And then at right angle."

If by chance this fallen trunk was that of the gum tree referred to, then we must turn at right angles, either to the right or left. This was utterly impossible, as we were encompassed on either hand by solid walls of rock. We carefully searched for an opening, but found none. Two of our torches were by this time exhausted. We wisely concluded to husband the remaining four. For a time the darkness was oppressive, but finally we were able to distinguish large objects. Jagga Jagga and I set to work constructing crude stone steps, by means of which we could clamber to the top of the fallen log. In an hour we had accomplished the task. There we were confronted by darkness on the other side, and no means of descent. Jagga Jagga climbed onto the slippery trunk, peered over, slipped and slid out of sight. I could hear his nails scratch as he clutched frantically at the slippery surface. In a moment he struck cat-like on his feet, and the next instant I gathered that he had not been seriously injured. In an incredibly short time he built up a stone work from his side, down which I passed with the remaining torches; one of which we lit. Then I consulted the greenstone disc. It had lost the power of pointing in any single direction, but oscillated with great intensity, and finally fell from the quartz pyramid. The experiment was repeated many times, but invariably with the same result. Glancing at the constellations above my head, I decided to await that critical hour, which, according to the parchment, would have some peculiar effect upon the greenstone. Not possessing a watch I could only approximate the hour by the position of the stars. As the time drew near my hands trembled, my heart throbbed and a clammy sweat bathed my body. Jagga Jagga shivered like one in the ague.

To avoid missing the coveted minute I constantly placed the greenstone on its pedestal, from which it constantly fell, after a few violent vibrations. Suddenly, in one of the experiments, it ceased to vibrate, and gradually turned over on its side, until the arrow pointed to the rock beneath our feet. There it hung suspended on the side of the pedestal by some powerful attraction for fully five minutes, then it fell upon its edge, rolled swiftly for a yard across the flat stone, on which the experiment was made, fell into the stream and vanished forever. As I nervously clutched after it Jagga Jagga gave a shout and clapped his hands with glee. The dreaded talisman had disappeared, and, with it, all tokens of fear upon the part of my dusky companion, who was at once anxious to explore the uttermost bowels of the earth, did I but say the word.

I examined the spot whereon we stood. It was a shelving rock some twenty feet wide, and in nowise differing from the formation over which we had passed for the last half-hour. The surface consisted of flat stones, lying in irregular masses, the edges overlapping each other. I pointed to these stones, which Jagga Jagga began removing and piling up in a heap.

Soon an opening about eighteen inches in diameter was visible. A gust of air from below nearly extinguished the torch, but finally subsided into a gentle current. Looking down I saw that the opening did not exceed two feet in depth, when it turned at right angles and ran in the direction of the cliff. Descending I found

PLUM HOLLOW. 103

that with great difficulty I could enter. I doubled myself up so as to enter head first. At my heels followed Jagga Jagga, gabbering with a loquacity which was in marked contrast with his former silence. After we had advanced a few yards the opening gradually descended and widened until we found ourselves in an immense vaulted chamber, from which ran a gallery fully thirty feet wide and from ten to twelve feet in height. The air was dry and warm, proving that there must be another communication with the outside world.

In the centre of the gallery we came, at times, upon little pools of water, but of no great depth. The walking was excellent, consisting of a bed of sand. An examination of this curious place convinced me that we were travelling upon the bed of an ancient river, long since gone dry. We searched in vain for any marks on the wall, which would be represented by the marks "o o o o o o o o" in the parchment.

They were no where to be found. The walls were of slate color. The last torch was lit, and we determined to beat a hurried retreat, when I stumbled and dropped the torch in a pool of water at my feet. It spluttered for a few brief seconds and then went out. In the darkness I felt my companion, who rushed to my side, clinging in nervous fear to my body. In the confusion of the moment I turned around several times, and then the truth flashed upon me that I could not decide which was the way out. We could only experiment by keeping on the bed of sand, which was the softest in the centre. For a time we thus proceeded, but with no sign of escape. Fearful of an accident our progress was very slow. Then we decided we had taken the wrong direction, and retraced our steps, with no better result. The fact that daylight would bring us no relief in our underground prison was disheartening, but finally, worn out and exhausted, we lay down on the sand and in half an hour dropped into an uneasy, fitful slumber. I was awakened by Jagga Jagga shaking my arms in the most violent manner, and at the same time striving to explain some discovery which he had made; but, such was his excitement, that I could make nothing of his words. He pulled me rapidly along, when, far away, I caught the gleam of a faint light. This was what the native, with his clearer eyesight had discovered. As we proceeded, the light increased, and in fifteen minutes we climbed a steep incline, parted some tangled bushes, and found ourselves on a side hill, in the morning sunshine. We carefully marked the spot, and then hurriedly returned to our camp, where, after a substantial breakfast, we determined to explore in a systematic manner, every nook and cranny in which Billa La Rue's secret was hidden.

We collected sufficient inflammable material for a great number of torches. I entered the passage and commenced my work. Jagga Jagga busied himself with bringing down materials for additional torches. As the dinner hour was approaching I sent my black friend out for provisions. Instead of going to the camp, where we had plenty of cooked meat, he knocked over a young wallaby, which he brought down and exhibited with the pride of a hunter. I told him to cook it. This he proceeded to do by building a fire in the cavern from the fagots which he had collected. My search had been fruitless and the chill of despair crept gradually over me. The wallaby was done to a beautiful crisp brown, and as we sat on the sand enjoying our meal I glanced into the embers of the fire. A shining substance caught my eye; it was a pure white metal, which had run out in little patches from the spot where the fire was the most intense. I gave a shout which rang through the cavern and sent Jagga Jagga to his feet with a bound. The mystery was solved. The marks "o o o o o o o o" in the manuscript represented grains of sand; and on this sand we had tramped an entire night. We gathered several small specimens of the metal and carried them out into the sunlight, where I pronounced the discovery silver. Then we collected a quantity of the sand in the skin of the wallaby. By constructing a rude furnace, with a bellows made from an opossum skin, we demonstrated, in a few days, that every grain of the black sand was a minute crystal of the precious metal. This fact proved, the charming oasis, which I had admired with the ardor of a lover, became a prison-house, from which I panted to escape.

BOOK II.

THE STORY OF LITTLE RUE.

A few days after the first remittance arrived from New York, Squire Mallory paid a visit to the Jahns family, where he held a long conference with the father and a short consultation with the stepmother. Rue was then called in and told that she was to have a new dress and boots if she would go to school during the summer. She pursed up her mouth and shook her head in a most empathic manner. Squire Mallory then informed her that if she would comply with the request he would buy her a beautiful box of paints and brushes and some pictures. Rue's eyes sparkled with excitement and then she said slowly, "I won't promise."

"Why?" inquired the squire.

"Because ma promised me a beautiful picter and brought me a pair of shoes. I don't care for shoes, but I do love picters, and you'd go and buy shoes."

"Oh, no," replied the squire, "1 will bring the pictures, and then you will go?"

"Yes," she answered promptly.

The next week, the necessary purchases having been completed and five small chromos delivered into the hands of Rue, together with a box of water colors, a few oil colors, with brushes, bits of academy board and some paper suitable for water colors, the little artist, tin pail in hand, which contained her lunch, hied away to the district school, where her arrival was hailed by a swarm of children, who at once set to work to make the life of Rue unbearable, as it was well known in the neighborhood that she did not know her letters.

"Here comes Rue Jahns," they shouted.

"Where did you get that new dress?" asked a redheaded romp with a pug nose and a freckled face.

Then the boys set up a shout of "Boots, boots, boots," for Rue was the only child present wearing any foot covering.

"What classes are you going in?" inquired Dan Polly's sister. "Are you going to take up geography and history and grammar?"

Rue answered not a word, but pushed her way through the swarm of human hornets into the log school-house, where she was followed by a pell mell rush of tormentors.

"Oh Jahns don't know nothing," cried a pert miss, "but let her alone, her pa is a snob and her ma sells cabbages."

Then the chorus yelled "Snob and cabbages, snob and cabbages."

The blue eyes began to open wide and flash. Not a sign of fear was written on that little face.

"Come up and say your lesson," cried Sally Polly, seizing Rue by the ear and attempting to pull her off the bench. The next instant Sally Polly was rolling on the floor, the blood streaming from her nose, while two great bunches of her hair were tightly clasped in Rue's hands.

"A fight, a fight—a girl fight," yelled the delighted boys. "Form a ring. Now, Sally, go for her," they cried, helping Sally to her feet. But Sally did not want to go for anything, and sulked and blubbered, while Rue faced her enemy with a courage which was infectious. Instantly the tide changed. "Hurrah for Jahns," shouted the boys, and every urchin nearly split his throat in response. The victory was complete. The biggest boy in the school declared that he would thrash any chap who in future bothered Rue Jahns. Then the mob rushed into the open air, leaving Rue and Sally Polly alone in the school-house.

Sally was crying as if her heart would break. Rue went over to her and whispered, "Don't cry any more, it hurts me."

Sally poured forth a fresh supply of tears. Rue sat down by her side, put her arm around her neck and said, "Please don't, the teacher is coming and, and——" Then Rue began to sob. Sally, who was not a bad girl at heart, in turn comforted Rue. The tears were dried, and in ten minutes the two were fast friends.

The artist, with her little hands, had won her place in the district school. A place which, from that day, she maintained without a rival. The boys gave her their hearts because she would fight; Sally, because she could forgive an injury.

At school Rue's progress was by no means remarkable. She learned to read with wonderful rapidity and to write a crabbed, angular scrawl. Mathematics were to her a sealed book, geography and grammer of but little interest.

Great portions of her time were spent in drawing pictures on her slate and in reading over and over again all the stories in the readers up to the highest forms. The teacher, who, very fortunately, had a vague impression that this little girl had not been cast in an ordinary mould and that at some time in the future she would become a famous woman. How or why this impression had been created she could not tell.

Nearly two years had crept by. Rue had grown rapidly in stature and gave every promise of becoming a beautiful woman. It was only a promise. She was light and willowy, the fleetest runner in the school, an expert oarswoman, for Squire Mallory had secured for her a small row-boat, with which she made excursions to the islands for many miles around.

Jahns paid not the slightest attention to her movements, while her stepmother had long since abandoned all attempts to interest her in the cultivation of cabbages. With no guiding hand her imagination ran riot. This was fostered by the fact that she had secured several works of fiction, which furnished her only knowledge of the great world beyond the rocky point on the St. Lawrence. The school she regarded as a penance, paid for obtaining pictures and materials with which to paint—a means to an end. During the long winter months she gave herself unreservedly to the creation of paintings and crude sketches. She had soon discovered that she could not draw with any degree of accuracy. Her lines were irregular and absolutely wanting in all that is necessary in a pen and ink artist. The cheap chromos, with which Squire Mallory supplied her, were to her the highest ideals of art, and yet she never attempted to copy them, though they were treasured with all the care which a connoisseur bestows upon a Rubens or a Turner. Squire Mallory's knowledge of art was extremely limited and, in consequence, his purchases were by no means calculated to give Rue any adequate conception of the task which lay before her, ere she could hope to earn even a livelihood by painting, much less become a great artist. The child had not entered upon the path from motives of gain or ambition. She was impelled to paint. She could not resist the impulse which drove her forward. It was born in her and, being the dominant passion of her existence, it laughed at obstacles and mocked at difficulties. In the realization of the thoughts, which haunted her by day and moulded her dreams by night, she experienced an exquisite pleasure; a pleasure only vouchsafed to the gifted few who hear in their soul

"The music of wondrous melodies."

Such melodies as the poet weaves into song, the musician into harmony, the painter into living, breathing song and melody, blended in colors and conceptions, which cannot die.

Rue's knowledge of color was intuitive. Instinctively she shrank from the inharmonious. The ugly hurt her with an intensity which was physical. She saw all that was beautiful in nature and labored to reproduce it. This faculty was developed in the highest degree. With closed eyes she saw before her a panorama of countless forms of beauty, flitting and changing like rainbow tints. These forms she in vain strove to seize and perpetuate. Therein she found her keenest disappointment. Strive as she would, they all vanished when imprisoned on the canvas. The curves and lines of beauty, which ran riot in her brain, were too illusive for her brush. The creative faculty she possessed; manual dexterity alone was lacking. Nature had made her a painter of the highest type. The fond old mother had clothed her soul with imagination, which her hands in vain assayed to transmute into tangible facts. Bitter were the tears this little artist shed over her failures. No critic stood by to point out her defeat; she felt it herself. Between her dreams and the reality the gulf was too wide not to be painfully apparent. Many and oft were the times when she threw down the brushes in despair, and vowed that they would never be taken up again. Why contend against such fearful odds? As she grew older a dim hope came that she might at some time go away to Italy, the home of her art, and under sunny skies seize upon the inspiration which would brush from her path some of the obstacles which beset her way. An inexorable law drove her forward along the track full of thorns and briars and defeats. She could not abandon it and sink into the commonplace. She was a sufferer, and yet, mingled with the pain, were at times sunbeams of comfort. When she compared her first crude efforts on the birch bark with the product of her brush two years later a faint smile lit up her face. She had gone forward on the road by feeble steps—but she had gone forward. Then she sighed as she felt that this same road stretched away into the infinite. Poor child! she did know that it has no end and that those to whom it has been given to penetrate the mists which hang over the hills where only genius may tread, see stretching beyond, vistas of which the child dreams not.

Half a mile down the river there lived a French

family, St. Pierre, a relic of the olden days when the tri-color floated over the citadel at Quebec. One son, who was a cripple, had, in more prosperous days, been sent to the seminary at Montreal, where he had received an excellent education which, upon the isolated banks of the St. Lawrence had proved of no practical value. Now an old man, the scholar lived only in the past—communing through the few volumes which he still possessed—with the men and events of La Belle France in the 18th century. With this old man, Rue Jahns had become a great favorite, and from him she acquired a knowledge of the language which enabled her to carry on a limited conversation in the French tongue. The facility with which she acquired a foreign language was simply surprising. George St. Pierre urged her to obtain a French Grammar, which she did from Squire Mallory, who had grown so fond of his protege that he frequently advanced sums when Martyne's remittances were exhausted. Rue set to work during the long winter evenings and within a few months her knowledge of French enabled her to converse with ease and fluency. Furnished by her lame friend with a few standard works, she gathered from them some faint perception of the usuages of society. Then it began to dawn upon her that she was a savage, and that the mere fact that she was an artist by nature would not enable her to bring about the changes in her surroundings, of which she caught brief glimpses in the future. She had resolved to go to Rome, though at that time she did not know in what country the Eternal City was situated. She did not breathe her secret. In one of the French works she had come upon a few brief pages in which

she caught sight of some of the art treasures to be
found on the banks of the Tiber. The Cistine Chapel
was briefly described in the book. She would see this
marvelous spot or die in the attempt. Once the resolve
was formed, Rue set to work to acquire the means necessary to carry out the plan. No circumstances could be
less propitious. She was but a child without money or
influential friends, with no knowledge of the world and
an education limited to a very scant knowledge of her
mother tongue and a smattering of French. During the
past two years a great change had taken place amid
the islands of the St. Lawrence. Fashionable society in
the United States had suddenly made the discovery that
while it had annually been rushing across the Atlantic
to spend a few weeks upon Swiss lakes, there existed
upon the northern borders of the Empire State a panorama of islands and rapids which put to shame in
beauty and extent the fabled resorts of the old world.
As if by magic there sprang up upon shore and island,
cottages and palaces, colossal hotels, parks and summer
resorts, with steamers and yachts and a flotilla of small
boats counted by thousands. The votaries of pleasure,
the seekers for health, the tired, the worn and the weary
found in this northern bracing atmosphere the rejuve-
nating effects which they so eagerly sought. During the
long winter days when river and hills and pines were
wrapped in snow and ice, in the little cabin on the
point, Rue toiled and painted sketches of foliage, of
Chimney Island with its ruined block-house; of Grenadier and Wolf, of The Three Sisters, of Jack Straw
lighthouse, of The Fiddler's Elbow, of Squaw Point
and La Rue's Creek. Under her deft fingers, these well

known scenes grew into charming bits, full of Nature's sweetness and loveliness. A breezy freshness and abandon lingered about her productions which rendered them inexpressibly charming and attractive. They were not gems of art, but in them Nature spoke. The old, old river told the tale of its birth in the fastness of the ice-bound forests beyond Superior; of its mad rush over Niagara, and its purpose to reach Mother Ocean through the swirl of the Cascades and the Long Sault. When spring came, Rue had a large number of small sketches and paintings ready for disposal. With the first tide of visitors at the Thousand Island Park, she determined to try her experiment. Arrayed in a neat tight-fitting dress, a broad brimmed hat and a stout pair of boots, she pulled away in her little boat for the head of Wolf Island. The distance was some twelve miles against the current. She rowed along with a light heart, for the Cistine Chapel and the Eternal City were before her beckoning her on. As she drew near her destination and saw the little pier crowded with fashionably dressed women and men, her heart sank. She landed her boat in a little cove, took up her parcel of pictures, which were done up in a brown paper, and walked slowly up the path in the direction of the hotel. Then, for the first time in her life her courage deserted her. She trembled violently, a great lump stuck in her throat, and it was only by a superhuman effort that she prevented herself from rushing to her boat and rowing away for home. She would have faced danger in any form without a thought of consequences. Half a hundred eyes were levelled upon her, peering inquisitively into her very soul. Then came the feeling that her coarse

PLUM HOLLOW.   115

dress, straw, hat and heavy shoes were marks of inferiority which plunged her fathoms deep into a new despair. Up to that minute she had been a child, now she was a woman with a woman's instincts. She felt that fate had left her an outcast, a pariah against whom all these butterflies of fortune would rebel. With artless innocence, she hurried forward beyond the groups of men who were admiring her flaxen hair, her deep blue eyes, her pink and white complexion, her brown, shapely hands, her lithe figure and her elastic step. All these they saw at a glance. The coarse dress and heavy shoes were unnoticed.

A group of ladies on the verandah caught Rue's eye and to them she hurried.

With trembling hands she opened the parcel and, displaying the picture which she prized the highest, said in a faltering, hesitating way, "Will any of you ladies look at my paintings."

The conversation ceased and one lady motioned Rue to approach.

Then several gathered around and carelessly turned over the collection, remarking,

"Pretty."

"Very pretty."

"Quite a gem."

"Not bad at all."

"Who painted them?" was the inquiry from a little woman with thin lips.

"I did," answered Rue.

From that moment not another word of praise escaped them. They lost all interest in the "pretty, very pretty, little gems."

Rue saw the change, but could not guess its meaning. Then addressing a stout woman with a Jewish cast of countenance, whose hands blazed with diamonds, she said, "Would you buy one?"

"I never buy anything from peddlers," was the answer given in a tone which froze the blood of the little artist.

"They always paint them themselves," drawled a young woman standing by.

As Rue gathered up her treasures, two great, hot tears dropped from her cheeks and fell upon her brown hands. The first penalty wrung from her soul by her own sex. The next instant a change swept over her; her combative nature was up in arms and a light crept into her eyes which boded ill for her tormentors.

An old maid, with green glasses and a form like a carving fork, come forward and in a falsetto voice said, "You are too big a girl to go round selling pictures. You should join the Y. W. C. T. U."

"The what?" asked Rue.

"The Y. W. C. T. U.," repeated the questioner.

"I don't know him," answered Rue, with the accent on the *him*.

"How dreadful," exclaimed the antiquated skeleton. "It is not a horrid man; it is the Young Woman's Christian Temperance Union."

Just then there burst in upon the group, like a cyclone, a beautiful black eyed girl with eyes full of laughter and feet so full of music that she whirled through the astonished conclave to the step of a waltz.

"What have we here?" she cried, catching sight of a sketch which Rue held in her hand. "Let me see it.

Oh, what an exquisite bit. Who painted it? You? What an artist you must be. I've excellent taste but no money, but Rob will buy it for me—my big brother Rob. Only a dollar? You must be mad! Ask him five. He's got plenty of money and not a stingy hair in his head. Come along. You won't sell anything here without (in a whisper) you have a bundle of tracts."

Then she hurried Rue along the verandah, down the steps and out upon the green plot, where she paused.

"Did you ever sell any of your paintings before?" she inquired.

"No," answered Rue.

"I thought not," she continued. "Let me tell you something. You can't sell anything to women."

"Why?" asked Rue in astonishment.

"Because you are much, very much too pretty. If you were as ugly as that old maid with the green glasses, you might sell a few, precious few, out of pity. You don't know the world, do you?"

"No."

"I do. I've been out two seasons. Now, if you were a young man with long hair and a die-away look in your eyes, you could go up on the verandah and sell a painting to every woman there, except the old maid, she'd take two, and three if you threw in a languish."

Then the merry, black-eyed sprite laughed and Rue laughed too.

"Rob! Rob!" exclaimed Rue's good angel, calling to a great stalwart fellow, dressed in a yachting costume, who was lazily puffing a cigar in a group of young men, "Come here this very instant."

Rob and his companions came forward.

"Here," cried the impetuous girl, holding up a sketch of Chimney Island, "is the sweetest bit of painting I have ever seen outside of Paris, and I want you to buy it for me."

"How much?" inquired Rob, fumbling in his pocket and not even glancing at the painting.

"Two dollars," was the reply.

Rob produced the coin and lifted his hat to depart.

"Hold," said his sister, "you young men want a souvenir of your visit to the river." Then, with her sweetest smile, "The artist," nodding to Rue, "can supply you all."

Rue opened her package. In ten minutes after she was the richer by twenty dollars, and her supply was exhausted, save one solitary painting.

Thanking her friend, deeper with her heart and eyes than with words, she prepared to depart, when there strolled into the group an effeminate youth dressed in the extreme height of fashion.

Rue held out her last treasure and said in timid way, "Would you like to buy this little sketch."

"Aw, my deah girl," drawled the exquisite, adjusting his eye-glass, "What is your chawge?"

"Only two dollars."

"I'll take it if you throw in a kiss, my deah?" he said, ogling Rue at the same time.

The next instant he was in the air, only his toes touching the ground. The giant Rob had raised him by the ear, at the same time exclaiming, "You cad! apologize to the lady."

I—I beg your pawdon, ten thousand pawdons, everybody's pawdon," cried the frightened dudelet.

Then Rob let him down, and in a moment he was gone. A hearty laugh followed him. Rob bought the remaining sketch, and Rue, after many thanks hurried to her boat and pulled for home.

She had met the great world for the first time.

The practical results of the day spent at the Thousand Island Park, stimulated Rue to renewed efforts and activity. Buoyed up by success she knew that her supply of sketches would be rapidly exhausted, and, as all of her hopes were based upon her ability to obtain funds from her sales, she determined to devote the early morning hours of each day to increasing her precious stock. With the first glint of the sun over the Laurentian hills she was at work sketching and painting bits of river scenery.

Later in the day she pulled away in her little boat to Round Island, Butternut Bay, or some other place of fashionable resort, through which, for a few brief weeks, surged a tide of tourists. Mindful of the advice given by her first girl friend she never offered her work to one of her own sex. Her simple, artless manner and kind, health-tinted face secured many purchasers, who carried away sketches, not as momentoes of the St. Lawrence, but of the little artist with tawny locks, whose smile was remembered long after the panorama of island and river had faded from their memories.

One afternoon, at Butternut Bay, she met a gentleman who examined very critically every picture in her collection and then questioned her as to her mode of painting them. Rue did not understand in the least many of the terms which he employed, but instinctively comprehended that, for the first time, she was face to face with an artist. Her stout little heart fluttered and answers came hesitatingly to her lips.

Mr. Percy, for that was the man's name, led her forward by gentle stages until he elicited the principal events of her life and caught glimpses of the ambition struggling in her breast.

Then he took her by the hand and bade her be of good cheer, telling her that he was an artist, that he lived in Brockville, and that when the season was over she must come and pay him a visit. He then bought her most inferior picture, gave her his card and wished her god-speed.

With the first breath of autumn the summer swallows flew away to the great cities, leaving the river to flow and shimmer in silence under the maples tinted with gold and green, which one by one dropped their leaves into the current bearing away to the great gulf. A few lovers of the beautiful tarried to bask in the sleepy, smoky silence of Indian summer and punt their canoes through the purple haze which hung over and around the islands.

For a brief eight weeks Rue's life had been a continuous round of hard work. After a morning spent in painting, she frequently rowed away for ten miles, made her sales and returned home by moonlight, tired but happy in that she had added to her little store. Now that the work was over, she drew a sigh of relief and day after day sat idle and listless in some sheltered nook, whereon the sun shone, watching the wild duck and the great blue cranes winging their way to the south. In the reaction ambition and anxiety were alike at rest. Once again she was the child of the river—the dear old river she loved so well. It blabbed to her, as it fretted by, songs of the icy north. Its little waves whispered, "Come down with me to the great sea and ride on the big billows away and away to a sunny shore, where beautiful pictures will tell you stories of the dim past, until your heart leaps for joy and your lips ripple over with laughter."

By slow degrees the spirit of unrest came back and Rue decided to pay her promised visit to Mr. Percy. A consultation with Squire Mallory resulted in a material addition to her scanty wardrobe. The dress, fashioned by her stepmother, whose hands were more accustomed to the hoe than the needle, buried the child-artist in a garment so fantastic and grotesque that the fairies dancing on each four-leafed clover laughed outright. When fully equipped and seated in the stern sheets of the market boat, she resembled a diminutive old woman taken from the eighteenth century; the illusion was only dispelled when you caught sight of a great knot of tawny hair, which refused to remain "done up" and in fluffs and locks and ringlets crept out over the white kerchief which encircled her neck. Rue grasped tightly a white calico bag in which were her savings, amounting to nearly two hundred dollars, to be deposited in the Bank of Montreal. Arriving in Brockville, Madam Jahns took charge of the treasure while Rue made her way to Mr. Percy's residence on the outskirts of the town. In half an hour she found herself at the door of a neat villa, built on the bank of the river and surrounded by her dear old friends, the whispering pines.

A few timid knocks brought the servant, who stared in open-mouthed amazement at the quaint little figure before her. Only Mr. Percy's card, which Rue held out, brought her to her senses, and Rue was shown into the library. A moment after Mr. Percy entered and instantly recognized her, despite her antique garb which amounted to a disguise.

"My dear little friend," he exclaimed, "I am delighted to find that you have kept your promise and paid me a visit."

Rue explained that the delay had been caused by the dress, which she touched with her finger as a devotee touches a sacred idol. To her it was something fearful and wonderful to behold, and the child was right.

Then Mr. Percy inquired how many pictures she had sold.

"Every one," was the laconic answer.

"What are you going to do now?"

"Paint more pictures."

"And what after that?"

"I'm going to Paris and to Italy to study, and say, Mr. Percy, do you think two hundred dollars enough to pay my way? I've got that in the bank."

Percy smiled and shook his head. "No, my little friend, that is not enough, but you will certainly paint beautiful pictures yet and go over the sea."

Rue sprang to her feet and clapped her hands. Her eyes sparkled and danced, and then into them crept a far away look, full of longing and tenderness, such as one sees on the face of a mother dreaming of a child beyond the seas.

"Come, my little friend," Percy said, taking Rue by the hand and leading her into the studio. Here, in confusion, were paintings, finished and unfinished, sketches and dashes of color, bespeaking artist dreams. On an easel stood a work which Percy had exhibited at the Salon. Rue stood spell-bound. Her color went and came from brow to chin; then there burst from her lips a cry of delight, painful in its intensity: a cry which awoke a responsive throb in Percy's breast, hurrying him back to vain hopes, long buried, to struggles against fearful odds. Rue burst into sobs and tears and clasped her brown hands in an attitude of prayer and supplication. As Percy stood by wondering, the child fell upon her knees. In the solemn stillness Percy thought that it would be sacrilege to break the spell binding the young artist to the infinite.

Then his artistic sense triumphed over the spiritual; he seized a crayon and on a bit of canvas attempted to sketch the upturned face at his feet. In vain! In vain! In the dreams of the past, glimpses of such a face had come to him, but only in dreams. The supplication, the devout faith, the implicit trust of the Madonna, mingled and blended with unwavering hope, rested upon Rue's upturned countenance, clothing it with a radiance almost supernal and angelic. A sigh of pain and disappointment, full of anguish and defeat, burst from Percy's lips. Rue opened her eyes and smiled, smiled because she was happy. Her prayer had received its answer. Over her came a great calm. Not the calm of despair but of unchanging confidence in what the future held in store for her.

When she stood up she was no longer a child, but an

artist, who saw before her struggles and the ultimate success.

One by one Percy pointed out the triumphs of his brush, the casts and sketches, the aids found in a studio. She was very quiet and attentive, full of admiration, but intensely inquisitive. Then she said, "Mr. Percy, how long will it take me to become a great painter?"

"Many years, my little friend," was the answer.

"I mean a *great* painter," continued Rue, her eyes blazing with an unnatural fire. "Not a poor little daub, but a painter that the world will worship because they can't help it."

"If the talent is in you it will come out," said Percy. "I believe that it is. Do you understand?"

"Yes," said Rue simply. "I know what you mean. If it is in me I will make it come out or die. Yes, die, and be buried up the river."

Percy smiled. The energy with which she uttered die convincing him that the child artist would unflinchingly face death itself rather than acknowledge defeat.

The precious time was slipping by. Rue had promised to meet her mother at the market in two hours from the date of her departure for Mr. Percy's.

With some plaster casts, a few sketches and a copy of William M. Hunt's "Talks on Art," all of which Percy thrust into Rue's hands, she departed, having promised to renew the visit during the winter.

Rue had been gone but a few minutes when the door of the studio opened and a tall man lounged in. It was Percy's most intimate friend, Van Lear Majeroni. Majeroni was of Italian descent but born in England and prided himself upon his place of birth. During Percy's course of study at Paris he had made the acquaintance of Majeroni in the Quartier Latin. The dissimilarity in the two men had led to a friendship which proved so strong that when Percy returned to Canada Majeroni found the gayest capital in Europe flat and uninteresting and suddenly decided to break the monotony by paying a visit to the backwoods of Canada. To him the northland meant a place of perpetual snow. When he arrived Percy was not surprised to find that he was supplied with a small arsenal to protect himself from bears, wolves and Indians, having read in *Figaro* a sensational account of the Red River rebellion, and so scant was his geographical knowledge that Manitoba and Ontario were interchangeable terms. He came to spend a brief summer, but found the St. Lawrence so full of beauty that he tarried until autumn and there were no indications at present of his departure.

He missed the Bois, the opera, the Follies and the Student's Quarter and in their stead found an old friend, the majestic river and excellent fishing in the inland lakes.

"Most noble and high priest of culture," exclaimed Majeroni as he entered, "how happens it that you are wide awake before high noon? Have you discovered a pretty model or drawn the capital prize in a church lottery?"

"Neither," was his answer.

"What is the news? There must be news, else why that morbid melancholy gone," continued the visitor.

"You have missed the sight of a lifetime," said Percy.

"Of course, I have. I always do; but don't I bear up well under the disappointment?"

"Seriously," continued Percy, "it would have appealed to your higher nature."

"Not a doubt of it," laughingly answered Majeroni. "My aunt, who left me all her money, always appealed to those feelings, but unfortunately never succeeded in finding them. While the hunt was on she died, else she would have discovered a vacuum and then the dance would have been up."

"It was an inspiration," resumed Percy.

"And pray in what form did the inspiration come?" said Majeroni. "Was it a new picture, a favorable criticism, or something in petticoats?"

"The inspiration was a child," Percy retorted with asperity.

"If there is anything I hate it is a child," was the reply.

"But a child painter. A young girl full of enthusiasm, guided by one motive, animated by one thought."

"Yes and breath smelling of onions," broke in Majeroni.

"I shall tell you nothing about her," Percy declared, as he set to work on a half finished portrait, while Majeroni slowly twirled a bit of Turkish tobacco into a cigarette, which he lit and smoked with a complacency simply exasperating. Then in a matter of fact way he inquired, "Who is the child artist?"

Percy freely gave him all the facts at his command relative to Rue, and then Majeroni strolled away, but did not return to the studio for a week. When he came in he said, "I've seen her."

Intuitively Percy inquired, "Who; Rue Jahns?"

"Yes."

"A Canadian wildflower."

"No, a Canadian nettle. But seriously, Percy, "Why don't you teach the child to paint? She makes some fearful daubs."

"But full of breadth and power," replied Percy.

"Granted, if you say so," answered Majeroni, "but wanting in beauty and finish and, to my untutored eyes, a painting without beauty is a daub."

"Take my advice and try to create a daub and when you have finished the undertaking you will have learned a very salutatory lesson. But to answer your question, it is absolutely impossible to teach a man to paint, much less a child."

"Then how did you learn?"

"I never did learn, and that is the cause of all my trouble," replied Percy with a sigh of regret. "I gave Rue Jahns my last copy of Hunt's "Talks on Art," but if you contemplate entering upon the study of art I will send to Boston and obtain a copy for you."

"Never mind," said Majeroni, "I will accept your quotations as correct. Tell me what this American paragon says and why you quote him as an authority when you studied in the French school and American art usually stinks in your nostrils?"

"I quote him because he was a great painter and at the same time a great thinker."

"Rare combinations," said Majeroni, bowing with mock gravity to Percy.

"A home thrust," laughingly replied Percy, "but where did you see Rue Jahns?"

"At her father's castle on the Canadian Rhine," Majeroni answered. "I was on a duck shooting expedition and sought shelter during a storm in the hut where Jahns, *pater* (who by the way is a gentleman), gave me a glass of excellent brandy. It was there I saw your prodigy and recognized some of your antique trumpery, from which I concluded that the tow-headed vixen, who refused to answer any of my questions, must be your inspiration."

"That vixen, as you are pleased to call her, will be a great artist yet and then you will be among the first to pay her homage."

"Very probable," said Majeroni. "I confess no love for immature buds, I prefer the full blown rose in artists as well as women."

Then the conversation drifted into minor topics and Majeroni's queries were forgotten by Percy until recalled long afterwards by circumstances full of tragedy.

BOOK III.

DAWNING LIGHT.

Rue spent the winter in attending the district school, studying French lessons with her kind old neighbor, painting on the stormy days when the snow swept over the point. She was the reverse of a methodical student. Her aversion to mathematics was hereditary, that branch of study having been the pet aversion of her father. She devoured all the stories in the school readers with avidity. Then she bethought herself of her father's library; a collection of dog-eared volumes, sombre and uninviting, which from infancy she had regarded with awe, not unmixed with contempt. In her crude way she had never been able to understand how one could be content to sit in a dark room during the glorious long summer days, as her father was wont to do, when near at hand were the great river, the dark murmuring pines, the wild roses and the honeysuckle, with Chitter and Rosa and the baby squirrels, all things of beauty—all speaking to her in a language without words, but no less a language, which her young soul drank in and interpreted.

One day she stole into her father's room, where he sat in the ingle, and asked him for a book. The request awoke him suddenly from the reverie in which most of his hours were passed. That any person at La Rue's should want a book he could not understand.

"Who wants a book?" he inquired in a querulous tone.

"I do," Rue answered.

"You?"

"Yes."

"Rue Jahns wants a book," he muttered. Then sollioquizing, "Fred Jahns wanted books when he was young. Fred Jahns got the books and see where he is now," casting his eyes about the cabin. "Buried in a snowdrift, camped in solitude." Then listening to Mrs. Jahns' rasping tones in the next room, he burst into a laugh and shook his head. "No, not solitude, ha! ha! I am not out of humanity's reach and I shall not finish my journey alone. Yet I am dead, only waiting for the resurrection, December 25th. I've turned into a hybernating animal; in a comatose state eleven months and three weeks living on the dry husks of the past." Then remembering Rue's request, "Another Jahns wants a book. Take it child," and he handed to her the first volume within his reach.

Rue seized the book and retreated into the other part of the cabin. The work was without a cover, and thumbed and annotated with queries and comments in the crabbed chirography of Jahns.

By the pine knots blazing on the hearth Rue spelled out the title, "The Jesuits in North America," by Francis Parkman. A more unlikely book to interest a child could not have been found in the miscellaneous collection of Fred Jahns. Rue read far into the night that wonderful story of devotion and self abnegation. There was much which she did not understand, and yet her young soul caught, as if by inspiration, the great central idea underlying the tale, magnetic in its simple pathos, sublime in its portrayal of love almost infinite, animating, guiding and sustaining these early martyrs. Night after night Rue sat by the blazing pine knots, following, in imagination, the footsteps of the pioneers of the cross through the Canadian forest, up from Tadousac to Villa Marie, to Saint Anns; ascending the Ottawa by rapids and swirling, rushing waters to Allumette Island and thence to Lake Nipissing and Georgian Bay, to that historic home of the Hurons, near Penetang. She pictured the great "White Cross" amid the flames of hostile camps, now advancing with the pride and pomp of conquest, now driven back amid the triumphant execrations of savages, drooping in the smoke of battle, prostrate beneath hate, but rising again and again from the ashes and carried forward, while the maimed and scarred champions chanted in the great forest the *Te Deum*. Confronted by Hurons and pursued with unrelenting hate by the Iroquois from the cornfields on the hills of Onandaga, the Jesuits' battle-song was "Mercy" and their guiding star "Peace on earth and good will to man."

The spell which the perusal of the book wove around Rue was not due to an exhalted religious feeling; it sprang from the vibration of another chord. Born amidst the humblest surroundings and left to grow up without a mother's love, she had been reared as the wildflower is reared, which takes root with briars and and brakes and noxious weeds on every side. The community forming her environment was not vicious but ignorant. Pressed upon in a daily struggle for subsistence, the sordid had driven into perpetual exile the imaginative, leaving no abiding place for culture and refinement. Rue had inherited tastes and instincts which were constantly at war with many of her surroundings. Her blood in every vein demanded a wider field and genial associations.

In earlier days these promptings drove her into communion with nature. She was the only mother whose breast beat responsive to the child's yearning heart. The forest and the river, the birds and the flowers spoke to her in words which the sordid, the mean and the selfish can never hope to hear, much less understand. Parkman's book opened new vistas of which she had not dreamed. For the first she learned that the heart is full of sympathy and love; that self is a grovelling worm crawling in the dust; that love of humanity is the highest type of a sentient soul. She saw, in the deep glades of the forest and in the corn fields of the Hurons, Le Jeune, Brebeuf, Jogens and Lalemont suffering torture and martyrdom in that dim procession of the past. Then there grew upon her by insensible degrees the conviction that she, at some time, would paint the story of "The Jesuits in North America." Out of these visions of the past came the preparation for the achievements of the future. Every spring the St. Lawrence is dotted with the birch-bark canoes of the Indians from St. Regis. Their rude camps are pitched upon the islands and promontories, while they halt for a few weeks, waiting for the ice to melt in the streams and lakes of the far north, to which they journey each summer, returning in the autumn. Heretofore Rue, in the vernacular of La Rues, had looked upon these children of the forest as "dirty Injuns," now they came as types of the past.

With the advent of the first Indians, she seized her brushes and began her work. She sketched the braves as they squatted beside the little camp-fire of the wigwam (for your Indian never builds a big fire), the squaws weaving baskets from strips of elm and tinting them with the juice of wild berries, the papooses bound upright to pieces of bark which stood about leaning against the trees. She watched the frail canoes crossing the river in the fiercest storms. She studied and depicted the painted rocks near Brockville, which bear upon their precipitous sides the picture of a great Indian battle, fought long ere the report of musket shot re-echoed over the blue waters beneath. Every gesture and pose of the red man was caught by her deft brush and portrayed with realistic fidelity. The child had determined to make the Indian her own. Her soul was in the work. She never painted the degenerate survivors of a fast disappearing race. From them she caught and imprisoned the fleeting shadows of an heroic past, now rapidly passing into myth and legend.

In painting bits of island and river for summer sale, she interwove brief glimpses of the nomads. The islands of the St. Lawrence, lying in the Canadian waters, lent themselves naturally as backgrounds upon which to depict scenes in which the wigwam, the smoke curling from the camp-fire, the bead-bedecked squaws furnished bits of color and life, adding picturesque effects. To these she united sketches of the French voyaguers paddling up the great river, with batteaux, shooting under the aspen leaves of the white birch and the dark green spruce.

On the first warm day in June a large marquee tent was pitched on Poole's island, a mile up the river from the point. The marquee was fitted up in a luxurious manner, with a double floor covered with eastern rugs, and embellished with a few proof prints, around which were arranged arms of various kinds, including rare weapons from India, China and Japan. The steam yacht lying in the little bay beyond had also brought a small upright piano. Two small tents were pitched near at hand, one to be used as a kitchen and the other as a camp for the assistants. The owner of the yacht could not be mistaken. Majeroni paced uneasily up and down the shelving platform rock, stroking his black beard. His deep set eyes gleamed with an expression best described as dangerous. This was heightened by the lines about the mouth which gave the face a cunning and half malicious look, only to vanish beneath a smile and an expression of complacency. That purpose lurked in his mind was self-evident. What that purpose was only Majeroni knew. To his friend Percy he had announced his intention of spending the summer upon one of the islands up the river, within easy distance of the fashionable resorts, and yet isolated from the horde of pleasure seekers. The morning following his arrival he sauntered up to the Jahns' cabin, where he made a bargain with Mrs. Jahns, by which she was to supply his camp with vegetables and milk. The price was quite liberal, with no objections offered by Majeroni. The arrangements concluded, he entered into a general conversation with Mrs. Jahns which soon won for him the best wishes of the vendor of cabbages, whose loquacity had been damned up during the winter months in not attending the market. Now it flowed fresh, strong and vigorous, like a spring stream. From her Majeroni learned that Rue was away to the Injun camp, in fact, she declared that Rue had Injun on the brain.

"What has she been doing during the winter?" inquired the visitor.

"Studyin' French with St. Pierre down the river, goin' to school, and readin' all night," was the answer.

"Will you and Rue pay my camp a visit at an early date?" was the next inquiry. "I have a piano and shall be delighted to entertain you, and now that we are neighbors I shall expect you and Miss Jahns to be my friends."

"Oh, we will come, never fear," was the quick response.

Then he bade her good morning and sauntered away to his boat and pulled for the camp.

Mrs. Jahns called frequently at the camp, bringing with her as a propitiatory offering the earliest cucumbers, radishes and melons. The music of the piano delighted her, and for her Majeroni was compelled to play for hours. Once in the tent it was impossible to displace her by hints however broad. In Majeroni she had found her first attentive listener from the outside world, and, in consequence, deluged him the moment the music ceased. Majeroni was like one of the unhappy spirits shown in a painting by a monk of the middle ages, who depicted the lost souls confined in a narrow valley. On one side the mountains poured forth hot flames and sulphurous smoke, driving the spirits to the other side, where they were met with ice and snow and intense cold. Life became simply an alternation from consuming heat to freezing, from freezing to consuming heat. Majeroni took refuge in the piano from Mrs. Jahns' tongue, when the piano stopped the tongue began to play. What he suffered will never be known. During the last days of the month a few straggling visitors made their appearance, they were but the advance guard of the thousands to follow, and in the main, disciples of Walton, intent upon landing the king of the river, the maskinonge. There were times when Majeroni caught glimpses of Rue in her boat amongst the islands, but the glimpse was only momentary.

On the fourth of July Majeroni spent the day at Alexandria Bay, where the usual celebration was held. The country folk gathered from far and wide to take part in the festivities. A central figure in a group of matrons from the Canadian shore was Mrs. Jahns, who related to her acquaintances how Rue had made her fortune by painting. Two hundred dollars was a colossal fortune to Mrs. Jahns. The wives of the small farmers and even of the fishermen had been accustomed to regard the Jahns on the point as poor white trash, in that they were poorer than their neighbors. This feeling had been intensified in consequence of the course pursued by Jahns, who never forgot that he had been born and bred a gentleman, and therefore he refused to hold any intercourse with his neighbors. They reviled him because he would not work, and reviled his wife because she did work. That Jahns' girl they cordially hated, but for what reason not one of them ever told. It was simply a legacy which Rue received from her father. Curiosity for the past year had run riot on the north shore.

"That Jahns' girl was painting pictures; yes, not only painting pictures, but selling them. Who ever heard of the like? Only think of it; tow-headed Rue Jahns finding anybody fool enough to buy her pictures."

To hear the story from Mrs. Jahns' own lips was a temptation which they were powerless to resist. There were shrugs and ominous shakes of the head as she proceeded. At a time when Mrs. Jahns was in the midst of her story she caught sight of Majeroni strolling past. Here was her opportunity, she embraced it by seizing Majeroni by the hand and immediately introducing him to all her acquaintances as her particular friend. Then was her triumph complete. Her neighbors exchanged significant glances behind her back, but unmindful of all, save that she was the central figure in the group, she walked away proudly with Majeroni, who bowed to the group and took his departure.

Once out of hearing he said, "My dear Mrs. Jahns, I have been anxiously expecting that you would bring your daughter with you to the camp, as I am deeply interested in her painting."

"Oh! she never can find time," was the answer.

"Is she here to-day?" he inquired.

"Yes."

"Then I shall have the pleasure of meeting her."

He bowed and passed into the Thousand Island House, as he saw approaching several gentlemen whom he knew.

As Mrs. Jahns walked away she shook her head and muttered, "I don't think he'll see much of Rue. She hates him. I know she does, but I can't see why; for to my mind he is the only real gentleman on the river. No airs, but a genuine gentleman with heaps of money and not a bit stingy. No real gentleman's stingy, not even Jahns himself."

Then she drew herself up to her full height and went forward in search of her late companions.

When Majeroni entered the drawing-room of the hotel he suddenly found himself face to face with Rue Jahns.

His greeting to her was cordial, polite, even deferential. As she held in her hand a number of paintings, he said, "Miss Jahns" (she started; it was the first time she had been addressed by that term) "I am delighted to see that you have some of your paintings with you, as I have a commission from a friend in Paris, who requests me to send him some sketches of Canadian scenery. As we are neighbors now, I have been waiting until I could see you, that I might execute my commission by examining your selection."

As Rue did not attempt to undo her parcel he continued, "Permit me," taking the collection in his hand to place them on the drawing room table. Rue would have preferred to have made her escape.

"They are so charming that I cannot come to a decision," said Majeroni, as he turned over the sketches.

When the choice was made Rue discovered that the black eyes of Majeroni were fastened upon her. The gaze was not bold, yet it sent a blush to her cheeks. Her womanly instincts whispered "Beware." She had experienced the same sensation when she met the man the first time. At the mention of his name by her stepmother it had returned with increased force. In his eyes lurked a magnetism which she felt boded her no good, yet a magnetism that might become irresistible.

She accepted the payment for the paintings, thanked him and ran down the steps, hurried to the river and rowed out among the islands, where she regained her self-confidence.

Rue was a child of nature with artistic tendencies abnormally developed. Transmitted to her from her father's side came longings for the beautiful, tastes born of the past, cultivated by wealth, developed by luxury from Jahns to Jahns. To the last bud on the Jahns' stalk, (born and reared amid poverty and ignorance) had been transmitted all that was worth preserving in two hundred years. Rue was a blossom, regal in its luxurious beauty, struggling into the sunlight amid dank shadows, where squalid meanness lurked upon every side. Nature only spoke the language attuned to her heart. To all else she was blind and deaf. In a crude way she had thought out the problem of her life. She was devoid of egotism and yet felt impulses urging her forward irresistible in their force. A spark burned in her blood driving her out from and beyond her surroundings. She felt that the future held for her comfort and hope. She had yet to seek happiness.

The first star shining upon her pathway was the memorable day with Carl Martyne. Next followed the revelations and awakenings born of Parkman's book. Therein she caught glimpses of human sympathy and the universal brotherhood. To these experiences had been added a new revelation born of the consciousness that Majeroni, while indifferent to her artistic aspirations and regarding her crude efforts with contempt, had a set purpose in which she had been chosen to play a part. What that part was she had no means of knowing. Her experience was too limited. The prescience of the girl was an indefinite presentiment that evil lurked in the black eyes which attracted and repelled her.

During the remainder of the day Rue avoided Majeroni, and as Mrs. Jahns insisted upon remaining until after the fireworks in the evening it was nearly midnight when they set out for home. The night was intensely dark, a mist hung over the water like a great pall. To the untrained eye the navigation of the river was a plunge into Erebus. Not a star was visible in the sky. Anon the Grenadier and Crossover lights shot a few struggling rays through the gloom, but these were finally lost in the increasing fog. The current ran swift and strong down the American channel, but Rue pulled away for the Canadian shore, confident in her knowledge of the river. The lights of the Bay faded away. The difficulty which confronted her was to strike the narrow passage leading into the Canadian channel and guarded by a high rock known as Old Bluff.

A few big drops of rain fell, followed by a puff of hot wind, which sank away in the darkness, the fog, increasing in intensity and clinging like a wet garment to the river, stealing noiselessly away. As Rue's boat shot into the narrow passage there fell upon her ears the puff! puff! of a small steam yacht. Instinctively she ran her boat to the side of the overhanging rock until the end of the oar touched. Suddenly the lights of the little steamer flashed out, and in half a minute it

PLUM HOLLOW. 141

was but a few feet distant, running at full speed hard on the rocks. Mrs. Jahns screamed. Rue gave a few superhuman strokes at the oars to avoid being run down, sprang to her feet and shouted, "Port our helm, port your helm, you land lubber."

The pilot, either half asleep or drunk, sent the wheel hard over to the starboard.

The little craft swerved from her course and dashed first into the small boat and then upon the rocks.

The crash of shattered glass, as the wheel-house went down, the rebound of the hull, a great lurch into blackness, a shout from the aft cabin, a swirl and a gurgle and the "Cygnet" was at the bottom of the St. Lawrence. The skiff was cut in twain, and Mrs. Jahns, who had been sitting in the stern sheets, was pitched, with half of the boat, thirty feet distant into the river. Rue had jumped for her life, but was caught in the under tow of the sinking yacht and only escaped going to the bottom by the most violent exertions. When she came to the surface, Mrs. Jahns (who had been supported by her ample clothing) was shrieking in the agony of despair. A few strokes brought Rue her to side.

"Keep still," Rue cried, "and I will save you."

Mrs. Jahns threw out her hands and caught Rue by the skirt of her dress.

It was the question of a few seconds when both would be drowned.

The terror stricken woman clung with the strength of despair. With deft fingers, and submerged half the time, Rue unfastened her skirt at the waist and the next instant Mrs. Jahns went down.

At that moment Rue came in contact with a small boat, which had rested on the hurricane deck of the yacht and was now floating about bottom upwards. When Mrs. Jahns came to the surface Rue seized her by the hair and pulled her to the boat, which she seized convulsively but her hands soon slipped off. Rue supported her and told her to spread out her hands and throw her arms as far up on the boat as possible, but it was only for a short time that she was able to cling there. Rue worked vigorously and finally divested her step-mother of the skirt of her dress, which she tore into strips and knotted together to form a rope of cloth. This rope she passed under Mrs. Jahns' arms and threw the other end across the boat. Swimming to the other side she pulled the rope taut, and thus supported Mrs. Jahns rode buoyant as a cork. Rue was about to lash herself in the same position when she heard a faint cry but a few feet distant. Quickly tying her end of the rope to the oar-lock, she swam out into the darkness, crying, "Here, here." No response came. Then Rue touched the half-submerged body of a man. He was not struggling violently, but in a blind, aimless way was swimming around in a small circle. Rue cried "Here, come this way. I have found the boat.

There was no answer and no heed paid to her request. Then she took him by the coat sleeve, to which he responded and swam along with her to the boat, to which they were directed by the constant cries of Mrs. Jahns.

When they reached the boat Rue passed the end of the rope around him in the same way she had treated Mrs. Jahns. When this was completed the man and Mrs. Jahns hung on the opposite sides of the boat like the bottles of John Gilpin in his famous ride.

When Rue heard the cry in the darkness, she knew that it came from Majeroni.

Now that she had provided for the safety of two castaways, she cried out, "We have a boat, we have a boat," but no response came. The other persons on board the "Cygnet" were buried with her in one hundred feet of water.

Majeroni hanging on the boat side was in a semi-conscious state. His mutterings were incoherent and wandering, and to questions he paid not the slightest attention. Rue knew that owing to the precipitous character of the rocks it would be impossible to effect a landing until they had floated down the river a considerable distance. Swimming to the end of the boat, she grasped the rudder post and for the first time rested from her labors. Slowly they drifted down the silent river. The water gurgled and lapped the sides of the boat. The mist rolled over them in great arches. Suddenly Rue discovered that the boat had taken upon itself a rotary motion. Then she felt that they were saved. They were in the eddies and but a short distance from Grenadier Island, but the difficulty was to decide in which direction it lay. Putting her shoulder against the stern of the boat she swam vigorously until her strength gave out. When she paused she noticed that the water was broken into small waves which were constantly growing larger. The wind moaned and sighed, coming in gusts betokening an approaching storm. The white caps began breaking in feathery spray; the boat tossed; Mrs. Jahns' screams and prayers alternated with regularity. Majeroni hung half lifeless like a log of wood and buffeted by every wave. Rue was compelled to exert all of her strength to maintain her hold upon the rudder-post. In a few minutes the storm broke in all its fury. First the wind came down and around from every point of the compass, catching up the water and tossing it into spray, then with a sough and a sigh it steadied in the east and blew a terrific gale, lashing the water into great, green, creamy billows. Next followed torrents of rain, with growls of the thunder king. Thus dashed and tossed and thrown about, the three castaways drifted, helpless and without hope. By times Majeroni moaned. The fury of the storm had silenced Mrs. Jahns' volubility. She had given herself up for lost, and, now that she was face to face with death, met the grim mower bravely. Several times in rapid succession Rue was washed from the boat, only to catch it again. She knew that a few minutes more would end the struggle.

Mrs. Jahns uttered a shout of triumph. Her feet had touched bottom. With that touch came back all of her old strength. She seized the gunwale of the boat and half lifting it, with Majeroni hanging on the other side, raced up the sandy beach towing Rue, and landed her cargo high and dry on the shore. Loosening the rope binding her to Majeroni she shouted "Rue! Rue!"

"Here," came the faint answer, for Rue was lying at the stern of the boat with her head on the beach and her feet in the river.

Mrs. Jahns found her, caught her up in her arms and carried her beyond the reach of the waves.

"Rue! Rue! Speak! Speak, child!" but Rue answered not a word. "Oh, my God, the child is dead, dead, dead!" she moaned, sitting on the ground holding Rue in her arms and rocking herself backward and forward.

Then there came a vivid and prolonged flash of lightning, revealing a long winding bay of white sand, the overturned boat with Majeroni lying by its side, the river running in mad fury beyond, a few hazel bushes, a zig-zag rail fence and a road running away beyond

Mrs. Jahns sprang to her feet. She knew the spot.

Over the fence went the woman with Rue still in her arms. She pressed her to her breast as the mother presses her first born.

Down the road at a swinging pace, keeping the beaten pathway as if by instinct.

Straight through the mud puddles and over the boulders and fallen branches raced the stalwart woman. As she ran the tears coursed down her cheeks and fell in hot drops on Rue's upturned face.

The brave woman paused not though she had covered half a mile in an incredibly short space of time.

Her heart throbbed and beat with an unutterable pain; not the pain of violent physical exertion, but the pain of womanly anguish awakened for the first time.

Up to that fearful night she had been a slow thinking, voluable, sordid vixen, mercenary and without sympathy; now she was a woman, broad and deep and tender of soul. The iron clamps of a life of toil were suddenly snapped and there gushed forth in that race against death all that is pure and holy and unspeakably sweet in the heart of woman. She felt that a great veil had been lifted, and thanked the Divine Architect that He had given unto her a child, though born of another woman.

"Let her live! Let her live! Save her for me!" she prayed. "Oh, Rue, my darling Rue, come back, come back!" for she believed that the girl was dead. She moaned and sobbed, but slackened not her speed. Then she grew cold herself with a chill at her heart, as if touched by the icicle of despair, and broke into a volley of abuse and almost curses against the cruel river which had robbed her of the only being she had ever loved.

A dog barked almost at her feet. She had reached a house at last. With fury born of despair she rushed against the gate, tore it from its hinges, then flung herself and her unconscious burden through the frail pine door with a force which sent her into the middle of the small house, where she shouted, "Help! Help! Help!"

Fisherman Thompson, his son, wife and daughters tumbled from their beds just as suddenly, all shouting and screaming, and wild with terror. The dog, savage and unreasoning, seized young Thompson by mistake by the calf of the leg, thus adding to the confusion.

Two minutes elapsed before a light was lit. Then Thompson took in the situation at a glance. The Jahns' girl was drowned and her mother had gone crazy.

Tenderly he took Rue in his arms and placed her in the warm bed from which his daughters had sprung.

Some brandy was forced into Rue's icy lips. The fire was lit, the women folks rubbed, Thompson elevated the arms and inflated the chest, for he had been present at many such scenes in his long life.

Mrs. Jahns sat on the floor swaying from side to

side, but uttered not a word. In fifteen minutes Rue began to choke and splutter like an expiring candle, and in ten minutes more she was out of danger.

Her first coherent words were, "Where's the man?"

"What man?"

"The man, the boat, the ——"

Mrs. Jahns sprang to her feet. The sound of Rue's voice had awakened her faculties. "Yes, the man, Majeroni," she exclaimed, "up on the beach, beside the boat, but I guess he's dead long afore this."

"What beach?" exclaimed Thompson.

"The sand beach," answered Mrs. Jahns.

Thompson lit the lantern, seized the bottle of brandy and was gone in half a minute, and was soon followed by the son and the unfortunate dog, which despite curses and blows was determined to see the night out.

Thompson found Majeroni beside the boat, lying where he had been dragged, but not unconscious. His mind was wandering. An examination showed that his left arm had been broken and that he had received a terrible cut on the back of his head. The boy was sent to the house for a horse and spring-wagon, and half an hour later Majeroni was tossing on a bed with a brain fever which sent him alternately to Paris, London and then tangled him up in a steam yacht, a row boat and a storm on the river, into which he was sinking ten thousand fathoms deep.

The following morning Rue and Mrs. Jahns were taken home by young Thompson, who proceeded to Mallorytown to secure the services of Dr. Lane for Majeroni.

Majeroni, after two week's struggle, so far recovered

that he was removed to his camp on Poole's Island. From that date he rapidly gained strength, and in a few weeks had completely recovered.

A diver sent down to examine the hull of the "Cygnet" found that the pilot had been caught in the timbers of the wheel-house and there met his fate. The engineer had died at his post beside the engine. How Majeroni made his escape from the cabin of the yacht will never be known, as his last recollection was a crash and the surging of the water into the cabin. From Mrs. Jahns he had obtained the particulars of what transpired while they were tossing about on the river, for Rue had not visited him during his illness. To Mrs. Jahns he proposed making Rue a handsome payment in money, but when the subject was mentioned to the artist she hotly refused.

"I will not touch his money," she exclaimed. "I only did my duty by him."

Mrs. Jahns in making her report so arranged that she, as Rue's mother, received two hundred dollars, but the fact was carefully concealed from Rue.

Majeroni's motto was, "What is to be will be and the fates will have it so."

This explained to his complete satisfaction his escape from the river, but in no wise changed the purpose which was paramount in his mind. He congratulated himself that it would be best served by the accident, and he soon congratulated himself that all things were working for the best.

Majeroni called one evening at the Jahns' cabin and found Rue at home. She came forward and gave him her hand frankly and inquired how he was spending the last days of the summer. Majeroni's face flushed hotly. With the impulsiveness born of his southern nature he kissed her hand again and again, and burst into an impassioned and almost incoherent volume of thanks, exclaiming, "You saved my life. I owe you everything. How can I ever repay you? Accept my admiration for your courage, my respect for the nobility of your character, my devotion for your marvelous presence of mind. My dear Miss Jahns, you have made me your slave. Henceforth you have but to command."

Rue in vain tried to interrupt him, but to no purpose. When he ceased, she said simply, "It was a fearful night, but I only did my duty. I was born on the dear old river and know her ways and moods. You owe me nothing. Let us drop the subject, I must away to my work."

Majeroni protested and implored, but the little artist was gone in the midst of his words. Could Rue have seen the change on his face as she turned away, she must have shuddered. The smile on the lips died out, the teeth clenched, two deep lines ran from between the eyebrows well up the forehead and terminated in tranverse frowns. Over the whole face there lurked a leer of baffled designs and gleams of an intense hatred. Determination and purpose were written in unmistakable language on his countenance when Mrs. Jahns came unexpectedly into the room. Instantly Majeroni's face changed into a calm repose. "My dear Mrs. Jahns," he exclaimed, "I have a project in my mind which I wish you to help me carry out. I owe my life to your daughter. It is well known that she is struggling to obtain money, with which to complete her art education in Europe. The mere pittance required I should not miss. Let me advance it. Call it a loan—anything —only take it. 1 would have made the proposition to Rue, but she even refused my thanks. To you I look for assistance in helping me repay a debt of gratitude."

Avarice was the normal passion of the woman's soul. During a life of toil and hardship and poverty, she had nursed and fed and fostered greed; not with any practical result, save the hoarding of a few dollars stored away in the savings bank and kept a secret from Jahns lest he should transform it into a liquid.

Majeroni saw that he had enlisted the support of Mrs. Jahns, and for half an hour they held a whispered consultation, which terminated to the satisfaction of both.

When Majeroni departed, Mrs. Jahns made her way to Rue's little apartment.

"Rue," she said, "Mr. Majeroni has made me an offer and I want you to accept it." Rue threw down her brush. "He says that you saved his life, and that he will advance you all the money you require," continued Mrs. Jahns, her eyes sparkling with satisfaction. "Of course you can pay it back when you get rich—that is, if you want to, but I don't see any reason why you should."

"Never," exclaimed Rue, with an energy startling in its intensity to the prosaic German, who could only utter, "Why?"

"Why," Rue went on. "Why—because I will not be under any obligations to him."

"Then why do you take the money from Squire Mallory?" retorted Mrs. Jahns with asperity.

"I know why and that is enough," answered Rue, a soft light coming into her eyes and a smile upon her lips. "Squire Mallory is a dear *old* man and I love him ever so much. But I don't love that black-eyed man a bit, not the least little bit, and I won't have his money, and I shall hate him if he don't go away and never, never come back."

"But you want to go and learn to paint."

"Yes, and I'm going."

"It would save a lot of time and hard work," insinuated Mrs. Jahns.

'And with it I should never learn to paint," said Rue, in a petulant tone.

"Nonsense, child. I don't understand how it could make any difference."

"I know that you don't," Rue answered. "Let me tell you, though I know I can't make it plain, yet I see it and feel it. Listen. I want to be free. When I wander through the woods and paddle from island to island I am free, and that is the reason why I hear the trees talk and the waves laugh. You can't hear them, because you have to work. When I hoe cabbages a long time I grow deaf and dumb, and then I have to go up to Billa La Rue's graveyard and wait and wait until it all comes back to me again."

Ain't you lazy?" queried Mrs. Jahns.

"Listen," continued Rue. "The birds and squirrels are free, and chirp and sing their happy songs because they are free. I am only a girl-bird, and I must not be put in a gold cage. No, no—it would wither me all up, and I would be Rue no more; but somebody else, not a bit the same, and then Rue would hate that somebody. Do you understand?"

"Not a bit," was the answer.

"But you must," continued Rue. "You must feel as I do, else you will never, never know what it is to be happy. You want me to take in a lump all the things for which I am striving and praying. I can't. The lump would choke me. Wait and they will come, but only in little drops, not in a great big stream. Look at the old river out there. It was not born a mile wide and ever so many feet deep. It was born in little, little drops, hanging on maiden hair ferns and blades of grass, away up in the north where the great hot sun could not find them. If it had it would have drank them all up and there never would have been any beautiful river. No, it only warmed them a bit, and then two drops married, ran together, that was their wedding. The pair, now a big drop, went on a wedding trip with other big drops and so they ran on and on until there was a tiny spring, where thay all stopped and laughed and splashed water in the bride's faces. After some play and a little rest they raced out in a little stream, which could not get over a twig and had to run around it, but the river was born, and all in good time it came down here grown into a mighty stream."

Mrs. Jahns sighed and said, "Rue, that's a fairy tale, such as my mother used to tell me when we lived in the Black Forest, but I say take the money."

Rue shook her head, but answered never a word, and Mrs. Jahns abandoned her mission, but secretly determined to obtain a substantial sum from Majeroni, which she did by creating in his mind the impression that once it was in her hands Rue's scruples would vanish.

As the summer wore away Rue redoubled her exertions in disposing of her sketches. Many of last year's purchasers came back and bought again. With the charm of the local scenery she interwove the Indian camp and canoe. The dream of her young life, touched by her deft fingers, came forth in the portrayal of the lives of the Jesuit martyrs. These ambitious attempts led her by gentle steps along the path where she was destined to triumph. Heretofore she had reproduced the scenery of the St. Lawrence. Now she created, out of the scenes with which her imagination peopled her teeming brain, at first only shadowy streams and forests, cornfields and wigwams, priests and rude chapels, crosses and baptisms jostling in confusion without order or method. They danced before her like the mirage of the desert, they haunted her by day and played sad havoc with her dreams by night. In vain she attempted to banish them, for they brought more of pain than of pleasure. The solace only came when one day she impulsively seized her brush and began, in a crude way, to give form and shape to the impalpable fancies and memories of the past. They took root on the canvas and grew as if by inspiration. In the foreground a great, crude, wooden cross beneath a drooping elm, whose branches almost trailed the ground. An elm, such as one sees at night, and at night only; full of sweeping curves and lines of beauty given to no other tree in the great North Land. A delicate priest standing beside the cross, with thin face lit up by the unquenchable fires of devotion and self abnegation. But one half of the face was visible by the light of the small camp-fire. In the dim circle where the light faded and the shadows lurked, the high cheek bones, with dim contour of face and the bead-like, black eyes of a score of savages who squatted on the ground. Out of the darkness imagination created a scene so weird and solemn that involuntarily you paused and listened for the tolling of the funeral bell. Such was the picture painted by Rue Jahns, crude and never to be finished. A few more strokes of the brush and its charm had fled. Its execution gave Rue inexpressible pleasure. It was the visible outcome of an invisible power, dominant in every fibre of her being. To this first creation others followed; all born of the past, clothed in mantles of the bye-gone, and breathing a spirit, which in modern times burst into a flame in the breast of Father Damian. These sketches were not offered for sale, they were sacred ties binding her to a purpose.

At the end of the season she found that her bank account had grown to nearly five hundred dollars. During the winter she painted but little, but was surprised to find, when she took up her brushes, that she had made a marked improvement. Her progress in acquiring the French language was phenomenal. She spoke with fluency and read *Le Monde* with ease if not elegance.

For weeks she debated with herself over the step which she had decided upon taking, and finally announced her decision to her step-mother.

"I am going away in a short time."

Mrs. Jahns' conscience smote her. Should she tender Rue the money received from Majeroni? No; she could send it if necessary.

"Going away, child. For the love of heaven, why should you go away?"

"Yes, I am going to Paris, and then to Rome and Florence and Venice," Rue replied.

Two weeks later Rue sailed from Montreal on the "Parisian," *en route* for Paris. She carried a kind letter of introduction from Mr. Percy to a well-known artist in the gay capital.

BOOK IV.

ESCAPE FROM THE DESERT.

Day by day my impatience increased. The discovery urged me to abandon the oasis, and, if possible, reach civilization, where I could ascertain the value of the mine. Jagga Jagga and I set to work preparing a supply of dried opossum meat, with which to begin our journey. I decided to strike out from the southern end of the oasis and travel in a south-easterly direction, in the hope of reaching the outlying stations, stretching northward in South Australia, for that colony is a misnomer, reaching as it does from the extreme south to Torre's Straits at the north.

By easy stages we proceeded for two days over the desert and found ourselves the second night on the confines of a great tract of malle scrub. The heat had been intense, and every drop of water was exhausted from the skins made from the tails of kangaroos which served us as water bags. In vain we searched the hollows for the precious fluid. Jagga Jagga crawled into the scrub and disappeared; when I attempted to follow I could not find an opening large enough to admit my head, much less my body. After an absence of half an hour my black friend returned, carrying in his arms a bunch of gnarled and twisted roots.

He came up and said, "Dinkee! dinkee!"

The word drink aroused me, for not a drop of water had touched my parched lips for hours.

Jagga Jagga held out one of the roots, but I shook my head. Then he thrust the end of a root into my mouth, and seizing it with both hands began wringing and squeezing it with a downward motion. Imagine my delight when a little stream of water trickled out upon my tongue. I at once learned the art of extracting the precious fluid, and in a few minutes quenched my thirst.

The next day was uneventful, and night found us on higher ground, where water was comparatively plentiful. The fourth day was one of intense heat, and at noon we sat down on the shady side of a great boulder. After a rest I climbed to the top of the rock and scanned the surrounding country. Away to the east I caught the faint outline of a row of small poles crossing the plain in a straight line and fading away in the distance. Calling Jagga Jagga I pointed to the poles and inquired what they were.

He shook his head. It was evident that they were as new to the savage as to myself.

We made a hurried advance, and had not proceeded half a mile when the wires running from one pole to another were visible. It was a telegraph line with small iron poles. Evidently we were upon the confines of civilization. When we reached the line, which ran north and south, we turned to the south. I shouted for joy, and set off at a pace which taxed Jagga Jagga's powers of locomotion to the utmost.

With the stoicism of a savage he made no attempt to ascertain what the line meant, only panting and casting sullen looks at the cause of such undue haste. Hour after hour we tramped on through the yellow-reddish sand. Night came down upon us, and in the darkness, fearful of missing the line, I was about to call a halt, when a faint light, half a mile away, beamed out. The next instant I was running at a pace which left the native far behind. A large bark hut loomed up. Through the open door streamed the welcome light. Without halting or a word of warning I rushed into the shanty, with my heart full of thankfulness.

"Saints and angels defend us," came from a deep recess, which held a bunk, at one side of the apartment, where a man lay reading by the light of a candle stuck in a bottle.

"Thank God! I am saved!" I exclaimed.

"Ship, ahoy!" came from the bunk.

Just then Jagga Jagga arrived and entered with the cautious tread of a feline.

"White man dead drunk, nigger sober as usual," resounded in a full bass voice from the bunk.

"Stranger," I said, "can I get something to eat?"

"Tucker? Oh, yes; plenty of it. Let the nigger boil the billy, and put out a pannakin for me. Now I think of it, I haven't had any supper myself."

Then mine host turned over on his elbow and went on reading. I soon found the larder, and in half an hour had prepared the first good meal which I had seen in nearly two years.

"Supper ready," I announced to the mystery in the bunk.

'Grub," he exclaimed, as he bounded out upon the earthen floor with the agility of an acrobat

s he stood before me in his pajamas I marked him

as a singularly handsome man, probably about five and twenty years of age, with dark, chestnut hair, curling about his ears in love-locks. His countenance was singularly frank and open, and his manner of a dashing, careless type, which proclaimed him a whole-souled fellow of the purest English type, and yet never seen in perfection, on its native heath, but the product of a life in places where conventionality is unknown and the habitual reserve of the Briton is thrown aside for the free life of the plains, the desert, or the mine. On his pink and white complexion was written English. When he came out into the light of the hearth-fire and for the first time caught a glimpse of my outlandish costume he burst into a hearty laugh, and exclaimed, "By jove! Whose's your tailor? Not Poole of Regent Street, I'll wager a fiver."

"I have been lost in the interior for nearly two years," I explained.

'Beg a thousand pardons," he answered, his manner and look instantly changing into pity and tenderness. "Let me welcome you back, old boy," extending both hands.

This kind act brought tears into my eyes, for my heart was big with thankfulness over my escape from the desert, from famine, despair and solitude.

"Pardon my stupidity," he continued. "When you came in I put you down for a lineman from one of the upper stations, who had by some means secured a bottle of square gin and swallowed it too quickly for his own comfort."

"Don't mention it," I said, wiping away the tears.
"But where am I?"

"You're on the line of the Transcontinental Telegraph System, running from Adelaide to the Gulf of Carpentaria, and connecting there by cable through Java to India. I'm Tom Moffatt, at your service, manager of this station for keeping the line in working order, commander-in-chief of four drunken linemen and as many niggers as I see fit to feed."

"I'm Carl Martyne, of New York," I answered. "Captured about two years ago by the natives when on a mining expedition, which set out from Perth, and this is my good man Friday, to whom I owe my life," pointing to Jagga Jagga.

"First good nigger I ever met," exclaimed Moffatt, seizing the black by the hand and shaking it until the native grinned from ear to ear.

Supper over, Moffatt unlocked a small valise, and with the utmost care opened a bunch of tin foil, disclosing a dozen cigars.

"The last of my stock until the supply train comes in," he said. "But let us celebrate your escape by smoking the weed of contentment. Light up."

How I enjoyed those cigars only the smoker knows. Jagga Jagga, though he had never seen tobacco before, snuffed the aroma with such evident relish that Moffatt handed him a cigar. The black joined the smoking concert with the gusto and satisfaction of a veteran of the Leidertafel. Moffatt insisted upon my occupying the bunk, and lying at mine ease I related to Moffatt the history of my campaign in Australia, only omitting any reference to the part played, in the discovery of the mine, by the greenstone and the bit of burned paper.

From Moffatt I learned that we were about one thousand miles from Adelaide, and that the supply train, which brought up the provisions for the telegraph stations, was due in two weeks. The next day he carefully examined the grains of black sand and the melted metal, uniting with me in pronouncing it silver. He advised me to say nothing about my discovery until I had filed my claim in the Department of Mines, assuring me that should it become known a rush would set in, and long before I could get back the prospectors would take up the whole oasis, and the speculators at Melbourne float a hundred bubble companies. A few day's acquaintance with Moffatt convinced me that he was a gentleman by birth and education. Why he buried himself in the desert I could got divine, as he vouchsafed no explanation. His disposition was as sunny as the skies above our heads. His duties were merely nominal, the labor being performed by assistants. No instruments were kept at the station, save a very delicate one, which indicated any break in the line. Hour after hour the messages from Europe and America flashed over our heads, and yet we were as ignorant of the outside world as is the African savage squatting beside the head waters of the Zambesi.

Our only consolation was the morning paper, which made its appearance, crisp and white, with uniform regularity. The *Argus* came up every three months in a bundle by the supply train. The papers were then sorted and arranged in the order of their publication and carefully stowed away. Each morning the one of the date most removed was brought out and read with the same avidity as if fresh from the press. However exciting might be the news, Moffatt never touched upon his reserve, and by this means enjoyed the luxury of a morning journal in the heart of this lone island. I soon discovered that Moffatt told a story with great dramatic spirit and force. There were times when I held that he must at one time have been on the stage, but this belief soon vanished, for not a quotation ever escaped from his lips. He was superlatively indolent, save when the line got out of order, then he instantly developed energy which never abated until the work was completed. His fund of reminiscences of colonial life and experience was inexhaustible. When the candles were lit and the linemen asleep he delighted in repeating tales of the early gold fields.

One night while we were discussing my discovery in the cave, he said, speaking with great earnestness, "Have a care, Martyne, don't build too much on it, the stuff may not be of any value."

Noticing that my countenance fell, for all my dreams of the future had suddenly vanished, he immediately bade me be of good cheer, saying, "I will tell you a story illustrating what pluck can do in this country, and I know you have plenty of that quality."

MOFFATT'S STORY OF THE BAND OF HOPE.

Let me tell you a simple story—a story of the past. In the early days of Ballarat, when the hillsides were green with the eucalyptus and the wattle, when the streams from Bunneyong flowed clear as crystal through the valleys, clothed with the brilliant wild flowers of the plateau, the gold-seekers came by thousands, toiling across the arid plains and pitched their tents upon the site of the young city of the antipodes. Millions were gathered in the shining sands. Hearts leaped for joy over fortunes won in a single day. But the end came at last. Every rocky lead, in which the yellow grains were found, trended toward the mountain to the west. The diggings sank deeper and deeper. The obstacles quadrupled, until at last in every mine the diggers found themselves face to face with an immense basaltic rock, and the lead was lost. Upon every hand the cry went up, "The gold fields of Ballarat are exhausted."

The miners sought new fields. The huts rotted and fell. Where once were thousands of hopeful men the lonely night wail of the dingo was only heard. The laughing jackass perched upon the ruins and laughed with sardonic glee over the fallen greatness of the young city of the antipodes. Men of science, learned geologists, European savants and American speculators came, shook their heads and departed.

That basaltic rock might extend for miles. Millions would be required to solve the problem and who could tell that after it was pierced gold would be found? Such was the magnitude of the undertaking that the government of the colony admitted that the sum involved was beyond the resources at its command.

When science hesitated the uneducated miners stood firm. All the gold found came from the direction of the rock. Through or beneath that barrier, countless ages ago, the golden stream had flown.

The working miners called a meeting, which was not attended by a single person who represented capital. At that meeting they formed a company, that name has passed into history, "The Band of Hope."

The original stockholders consisted of about forty working miners, strong in hope, with sinewy hands, broad shoulders, but no money. They decided to go back on the plateau for half a mile and sink a shaft through the rock.

"What will it cost?"

"We do not know."

"When will it be completed?"

"We cannot tell."

Rough drawings were made, showing the trend of the various gutters which had been worked and the point at which they would centre, if extended.

One bright morning the "Band of Hope" met on the plateau. A claim was marked out and registered. Then a sturdy miner took up a pick and struck the first blow. That blow still re-echoes through Australia and its reverberations continue to be heard in Europe and America.

It was the signal of the emancipation of the masses. Not by the dreams of Rousseau, not by the community of Robert Dale Owen, not by the the logic of John Stuart Mill, not by the sword of Washington, not by the fiery eloquence of Gambetta, not by the stately measured periods of Gladstone, not by war or fraud or force, but by the UNION OF LABOR.

The incredulous smiled, as only the incredulous can smile.

The scoffers jeered.

The all-knowing derided.

The miners worked.

Nearly every member of that "Band of Hope" was a married man. How was the shaft to be sunk and wife and children cared for? Each man pledged himself to do two days' work each week in the mine or to furnish a substitute. They labored at other occupations for four days and spent two in their own mine. They tramped to distant fields and remitted money to hire other men. They toiled at home hours after having completed a days' work abroad. They formed parties and trudged to the ranges, beneath a tropical sun, and cut the timber with which to secure the shaft, and dragged it to the mouth of the pit. They constructed rude buckets from the native gum trees, which are almost as hard as iron. They built windlasses. They shaped rude cars to carry away the debris. They formed and fashioned, invented and contrived, as miners never did before. Foot by foot the adamantine rock gave way. One, two, three hundred feet they slowly burrowed. The public said that they were mad, that they were digging their own graves, but they faltered not. Perseverance was their motto, and hope their guiding star. Pressed upon by poverty and want the struggle for existence grew in intensity. Year by year crept slowly by. The clock of time stayed not. Hot winds from the interior of this then unknown continent bronzed their cheeks; their hair silvered and their forms grew less robust. Death laid its inexorable hand upon one by one of that "Band of Hope."

On a memorable day, never to be forgotten, the news run through the hamlet and spread itself over the great southern continent, that the end had come. The miners had pierced through the rock and struck—not the gold so long sought, but a subterranean lake of liquid mud. Examination proved that this lake was sixty feet in depth. It could not be pumped dry and it could not be avoided. What the basaltic rock was to the original miners the same was the lake of mud to the "Band of Hope."

The surviving members of the Band met one night at a little cabin accompanied by their wives. The men declared that nothing more could be done and the shaft must be abandoned.

It was the supreme moment.

The hush of despair was upon them. Strong men wept.

In the brooding silence a woman said :

"The work must go on."

"How?"

"Increase the number of days' work each week from two to four, plan, invent, contrive, put the shaft down through that lake."

"How can our wives and children live?"

"We can wash and sew, we can spin and weave, we will not see you fail."

What a cheer went out on the night air then.

In all the broad world of heroism by camp-fire or on the field of battle, by early Christian or modern hero, no greater tribute has ever been paid to woman.

On the flag of the "Band of Hope" was then written *cannot fail*. For two years the men built coffer-dams and invented new casings. They all ended in a disaster. Well could the poet sing :

"They build, they build, but they enter not in."

The reward came, as it always comes to those who will not surrender. One of the men invented a casing which overcame every obstacle. This was the second gift to humanity from the "Band of Hope."

Once upon the bottom of the lake, they again assaulted the basaltic rock with renewed vigor. Hundreds of feet beneath the surface they toiled, the blue strip of sky above diminishing day by day, month by month and year by year. The clang of pick and drill brought to their ears only the mocking echo of the frowning rock which encompassed them on every side. One evening as the miners were doing the last strokes of their daily toil, a pick struck through into the earth.

With the frenzy of mad men they clutched their hammers and delved, speaking not a word. Were they upon the confines of another lake?

Their drills rang out upon their old enemy, the rock, now crumbling and falling.

An opening was made.

With eager hands they dug into the earth and holding it up to the flickering candle-light saw the shining gold.

They had struck the great gutter, the mother of the mines at Ballarat.

For weeks fifty thousand dollars worth of gold came up from that shaft every night.

Tom Moffatt's story gave me increased confidence in my discovery in the oasis.

Three weeks after my arrival we were awakened one morning by, "Cooee! Cooee!" and a tramping of many feet around the hut door.

"Here they are," cried Moffatt, springing from his bunk.

A dozen snarling kangaroo dogs came bounding in, fighting and yelping over our black boys, who always slept on the earthen floor. I dashed out into the open air and found myself surrounded by laden camels and men on horseback. At the sight of the camels I rubbed my eyes in astonishment, as I was ignorant of the fact that the "Ships of the desert" were employed in Australia.

"All well?" queried the leader of the expedition.

"All well," answered Moffatt.

"King is dead," continued the captain.

"Tom King?"

"Yes."

"What was the trouble?"

"Shot in the thigh with a poisoned arrow by a nigger. Better have an eye out around here, Moffatt, may come up this way. You must send a lineman down there to give them a hand, it is only fifty miles."

"Poor King!" sighed Moffatt. "My next door neighbor on the line. Leaves a wife and family in Adelaide, don't he?"

"Yes."

"Put me down for a fiver on the subscription."

"Right you are, old man."

"Come in."

In came the captain, bringing with him two letters and a bundle containing the coveted daily papers.

While Moffatt was reading his letters my heart grew inexpressibly sad. When would tidings come to me from over the sea? Where was little Rue and Chitter and Rosa and how was Jahns *pere*? A thousand such thoughts came and went as I sat brooding in the bark hut that misty morning.

That was a busy day at the station, getting in the supplies, as the train was going further north. Moffatt arranged with the captain that I was to be taken down to the outlying settlement when he set out for Adelaide.

When the cavalcade returned I was ready for the journey. Clad in Moffatt's best suit and with twenty pounds in my pocket, which he pressed upon me, I departed, much to the satisfaction of Jagga Jagga, who had tired of the monotony of life at the station. The certainty of having breakfast the next morning always impaired his appetite and depressed his spirits. Moffatt exacted from me a promise that I would return with the mining expert, who was certain to be sent up to examine the mine.

Our journey to the settlement was uneventful. Arriving at an outlying township, I bid good-bye to the captain, purchased Jagga Jagga a suit of clothes, and mounted the stage coach *en route* for the nearest railway station, distant nearly one hundred miles. It was in January and consequently exceedingly hot.

I secured an inside seat, but Jagga Jagga fearing an accident, climbed upon the box with the driver. The road lay through a forest of dead gum trees, forming a landscape gloomy and monotonous. Such a scene is only to be found in this land of the dawning, where the sheep-farmer never cuts down a tree to clear the land but rings the bark to kill the tree, leaving the eucalypti gnarled and twisted, stripped of foliage, with its bark flapping in the wind. The European colonist landing in

America or Australia is animated by a tiger-like hatred of the beautiful forest, forgetting in his hatred that SHE is the mother of rains.

We had not proceeded a mile before the coach suddenly pulled up and the driver shouted:

"Nigger has shed his boots."

I looked back and there in the dust behind us were Jagga Jagga's new boots."

I called to him to go and fetch them, but he was suddenly seized with an amazing stupidity, so I was compelled to go myself.

Away we galloped again to make up the lost time, for your Australian coach is driven at a spanking pace, unmindful of the fact that in the back blocks there are no roads, only a track winding in and out through the gum trees.

Half a league went by.

"Whoa!" cried the driver.

"Nigger has shied his coat."

True enough the coat was behind while the cause of all this trouble sat grinning on the box, paying not the least attention to my command to get the garment.

Again I descended and brought back the coat.

I was beginning to get hot myself. Crack went the whip, round flew the wheels, up rose the dust in a cloud only known to this land. Ten minutes later the brake creaked and grated harshly and up came the coach with a round turn.

"Hello, inside!" shouted the driver now frantic with rage.

"Nigger's got his shirt off."

I jumped out and found Jagga Jagga and the driver

struggling with the garment which finally fluttered to the ground at my feet.

"Take him inside," roared the driver. "I won't have him here any longer." But the black moved not an inch.

"The dreadful, horrid creature shan't come in here," shrieked the only woman passenger, an aged spinster who had been sent out to Australia to convert the heathen.

Jagga Jagga put on the shirt after I presented him with two cigars and the driver grew calm at the sight of a five shilling piece.

We changed horses at a small township, but were not clear of the town when a furious struggle again broke out on the box.

"Nigger trying to get his trousers off," shouted the driver.

"Hotty, hotty, hot," roared Jagga Jagga in pigeon English.

"This is disgraceful, simply disgraceful," sobbed my inside companion, in tears. The fresh horses, with no hand to check them, for driver and nigger were clenched in a desperate struggle, bounded forward at a pace which set the coach swaying from side to side. I thrust my head out and shouted in vain to all the cause of the trouble. The next instant Jagga Jagga and the driver rolled from the box into the road. The horses sprang into a run, but fortunately the lines became entangled in the wheel and we came to a sudden stop. Much to my disgust I was compelled to finish the journey on the box for the double purpose of keeping raiment on the black and peace between him and the driver.

At Adelaide I called upon Sir John Elder and exhibited the grains of sand and the melted metal.

"Is it silver?" I inquired.

"No."

"Of any value?"

"Yes."

"What is it?"

"Tin."

"Will it pay to mine it?"

"That depends upon quantity and location."

Then I described to him the appearance of the cave and the large quantities of sand visible.

"This is highly important, if proved to be true," he answered.

My claim was duly registered in the Department of Mines, and in a few days a mining expert and two surveyors were detailed to proceed with me to the oasis and examine the property. Our arrangements were soon completed, and again I found myself *en route* for Tom Moffatt's station, where we arrived in excellent health and spirits. My welcome was a cordial one, and during the evening my friend informed me that he had decided to send in his resignation and return, after a few months' travel in the colonies, to England. I hailed his decision with rapture and proposed that as soon as the mine was sold we become a party of two, to which he assented. After a halt of two days we started for the oasis. The course had been well marked and we experienced no difficulty until we entered upon the desert proper. Here all traces were rapidly lost. The shifting sands had covered up the line of stones, leaving to my eye not a trace behind. Up to this time Jagga

Jagga had paid not the slightest attention to the finding of the trail, busying himself with firing a revolver—which I had purchased in Adelaide—at rabbits, wallabys, native bears and cockatoos, but never injuring any of them. As we halted irresolute and undecided the black Nimrod came up and grinned at our stupidity. Handing the coveted revolver to me, he began circling around us, gradually extending the diameter of the circles. Suddenly he halted and then set off in a straight line. Thus he trotted along mile after mile, only pausing for a brief half minute at any one time and never in doubt as to the course which would lead us to the oasis. He had developed in the highest degree the art of tracing and following a trail, of which not the faintest sign can be found by any white man. In all of the Australian colonies this gift has been utilized by the Government in securing the services of "black trackers" to hunt down criminals.

Arriving at the oasis we pitched camp, and the surveyors and expert set to work making their examinations and securing the data for their report. One thing was assured, the tin deposits existed and the quantity was very great. On our return to the station I arranged to remain in Adelaide until Tom's arrival. On our way down to the settlement we were surprised to meet, at first parties of two and three men, then a dozen, and finally cavalcades of half a hundred, with bullock teams and complete outfits. The secret was out. A tin field had been discovered in the interior. A rush had set in. The prospectors were going up to find the coveted oasis and stake out their claims. When we mentioned the desert and the scarcity of water they laughed and pushed on,

In a rush, death in its most ghastly form cannot bar the swelling stream of humanity. Men lie down and die by the wayside, they perish for want of food, they wander in great circles day after day searching in vain for water. A few weak-hearted and cautious turn back ere it is too late, but the great tide sweeps on, an irresistible wave, overcoming every obstacle, surmounting every difficulty and at last solving the problem.

At Adelaide, on the publication of the Government report, I was besieged by capitalists, speculators, syndicates and adventurers, all anxious to secure an interest in the new mine. To avoid any delay and obtain a competency free from any chance, I disposed of all my interest, save one-sixteenth, which I transferred in trust to Sir John Elder, to be held for Jagga Jagga. With forty thousand pounds safely lodged in the Bank of Australasia life took on many new charms.

Much to my surprise I was awakened one morning by a loud knock at my door and the musical voice of Tom Moffatt demanding admittance.

"I thought you a thousand miles from here," I exclaimed.

"Got my discharge a fortnight ago, abdicated at once and came down with a mining supply train on its way back from the oasis. No more solitude up the country, every back block swarming with miners, sharers and sundowners. What about the mine?"

"Sold out."

"Delighted. How much?"

"Forty thousand and a plum in the box for Jagga Jagga."

The light of hope in Tom's eyes, the breezy freshness of his conversation were in pleasing contrast to the languor and lassitude which marked his life at the station.

"Down at the Port I just met two old friends, Harry and Fred White," said Moffatt. "They are going up to their father's run on a kangaroo hunt to-morrow and asked me to join them. Told them I had a friend. Bring him along, was the reply. Fine station, charming old man, two pretty daughters, good hunting, best of wine, what more can you ask?" said Moffatt, out of breath.

"The programme is complete and I will go. When do we start?"

"To-morrow at nine, from the railway station."

We were at station at the hour.

The White brothers were young Australians, lithe of limb and overflowing with animal spirits; charming companions, with a dash which quite captivated me.

The run was through vineyards and orange groves and then out into the open country, past thousands of acres of wheat lands. At Vandalee, a wayside station, we left the train and were met by a groom with a drag and four thoroughbred horses.

I shall never forget that ride. Fred White took the reins. The four-in-hand galloped away like mad through the bush, with no well defined road; under drooping fern trees, whose fronds swept our faces; around fallen logs, down into gullies and up the sides of ravines we swept with a rush which set the drag swaying and rocking, tilting and jumping, but the speed never slackened until we came to a halt before a long, low wooden structure built of split palings, standing in creeping vines clambering up the broad balconies and festooning the galvanized water tanks.

Mr. White received us as only the Australian squatter receives his guests, while his two charming daughters joined with their father in making us at home. At dinner we made the acquaintance of the Rev. George Lilbool, a young clergyman sent out to the bush on a mission, he informed us. Squire White had built a small chapel on the station in which services were held monthly by the curate, whose spiritual field extended over a large tract of country. Mr. Lilbool was a graduate from an English university, with weak eyes, a timid and hesitating manner, and a drawl in his voice, which, to my American ears, was inexpressibly amusing. His congregation, he informed us, consisted of the squatter's family, the roustabouts and shepherds, an occasional sundowner and the families of the cockatoo farmers who had selected small holdings, much to the disgust of the reigning squatters. The second course was not finished when I concluded that the Rev. George was most assiduously cultivating a mission-field which was made up of Miss Rosa's affections. The merry twinkle in the eyes of her brothers and the smile playing around the lips of her sister, when the curate bent in respectful adoration before that mission, led me to believe that others had made the same discovery.

"I am delighted to see that you are taking a deep interest in the success of the mission, Rose," remarked Fred, with a profound bow to his sister. The color on her face deepened a shade.

"She is indeed a willing worker, would that many

more would follow her example," interjected the curate, his face beaming with satisfaction.

"Why don't you enlist Bell's services?" inquired Fred with a mock gravity, which all noticed save the infatuated curate.

"Ah, yes, but weally Miss White has not the time to spare. Her household duties are too exacting, and it would, it weally would be too much to expect the active assistance of more than one member of the family."

"Then Harry and I are excused," said Fred, laughing.

"Oh no, do not misunderstand me, the vineyard is large, too large (with a sigh). I shall expect you at the chapel on Sunday."

"I promise you that Harry and I will be there," was the reply.

"I want to awaken the public conscience among my parishioners," continued the curate.

"The best way to accomplish that," continued Fred, "will be first to awaken public interest in the work. Harry and I will exert ourselves among the young people and see if they can't be got out next Sunday."

The curate bowed his thanks.

Mr. White smiled with satisfaction and Moffatt looked surprised. After dinner Tom and I strolled into the garden and took our seats in a small summer-house. In a short time Fred White and his youngest sister passed by and we caught fragments of a conversation.

Rose.—"I tell you, Fred, he is becoming unbearable."

Fred.—"Then let the heathen perish."

Rose.—"I shall be compelled to abandon the station and flee from"—

Fred.—"The wrath to come."

Rose.—"For once try and be sensible and advise me."

Fred.—"I fear that your zeal in the mission——ary is growing lukewarm."

Rose.—"I shall not say another word."

Then they passed out of hearing. "Parson bady hit," remarked Moffatt. "There will be music in the air here shortly, shall we stay and listen to it?"

"No," I answered, "on Saturday we will run down to the city."

For three days we hunted kangaroo. The sport was excellent and left nothing to be desired. Saturday morning I announced my intention of taking my departure. The entire family united in a protest, and then Fred called me to one side and said, "You must not go, there is to be a grand hunt Sunday, the whole country-side will be out. It will be the chance of a lifetime."

But we have all promised to attend church," I answered.

"And so we will. Yet I promise you will see the old man kangaroo treed."

Then I consented to remain.

The White brothers were not down for breakfast Sunday morning. Moffatt and I concluded that they were away on the hunt, but we said nothing.

Half an hour before it was time to start for church we saw them ride into a paddock and dismount. It had rained the night before and they were bespattered with mud from boots to chin and evidently hard pressed for time, as they hurried into the kitchen and disappeared.

Fifteen minutes after they were on the lawn, scrupulously dressed and ready for church, to which the family immediately proceeded.

As we strolled along I said to Fred, "How did the hunt come off?"

"Not on yet," was the answer. "You will see the promised fun."

The grove surrounding the chapel convinced me that the fame of the curate, as a preacher, had spread far and wide. A horse was tethered to each tree and bush. Our entrance was the signal for a general rush to secure seats, only a few of which were occupied by families of the cockatoo farmers. Behind us streamed a motly assemblage, which filled every seat and also blockaded the aisles in the vicinity of the door.

The Rev. George Lilbool's face beamed with satisfaction. The squire's pew was well up to the front, and on the right, so that an excellent view of the congregation was secured from where we sat. The great majority were young men, sunburned brown, with immense cabbage-tree hats and many grasping firmly their stock whips with lashes twenty feet long. Boys were present in great numbers, their clothes splashed with mud and their faces pictures of good nature and robust health.

The service commenced.

All joined heartily in the responses. The attention was all that could be desired.

The second lesson was over and the curate began the sermon.

At that moment there floated through the open door the mellow notes of English fox hounds in full cry.

Squire White moved uneasily and cast a searching glance upon his sons, but not a muscle of their faces moved, they were listening intently to the sermon.

A smile ran rapidly around among the young men. The sedate cockatoo farmers frowned.

The curate proceeded with his sermon as the cry died away in the distance. Then it burst forth again, nearer, clearer than before.

The curate paused, an angry flush mantling his face.

Mingling with the long notes of the fox hounds came the short, sharp bark of the kangaroo dogs.

Tom Moffatt seized a prayer book and suddenly became interested in the creed.

Again the cry died away and again the Rev. George proceeded, but only for a short time.

The pack in full cry again drew near, and mingling with the louder notes of hound and kangaroo dog I caught the snarl of mongrels, great and small, bringing up the rear.

It was a hunt indeed, and all the dogs were out.

To the rear of the chapel the pack swept.

A faint color came into the curate's face, for under the trying ordeal he had grown deadly pale.

Suddenly the cry boomed out again with redoubled volume and distinctness.

The sermon was lost, but the curate did not surrender without a struggle.

"My beloved friends, the mission——"

"Yelp! Yelp! Yelp! Yelp!"

"My beloved friends——"

"Yelp! Yelp! Yelp!"

"My beloved——"

"Yelp! Yelp!"

"My——"

"Yelp!"

Six fox hounds leading the van, half a hundred kangaroo dogs, and as many more pointers, terriers, black-and-tans and a solitary poodle burst into view not a hundred yards away.

The church-wardens sprang to their feet to close the door.

In vain.

The young men blockaded every aisle. They swayed from side to side, every face lighted up with enthusiasm, but not a foot moved.

The line of dogs was strung out like a frayed and ragged rope, with a big fox hound at the head and the poodle at the tail.

Straight on they came.

Every person sprang to his feet.

There was a mad rush of dogs at the door. The young men parted in the centre aisle as if by magic and the next instant half the pack were inside, barking, yelling, snarling, all striving to reach the parson.

What the curate thought I never knew. He acted, and in the twinkling of an eye mounted the pulpit, shouting, "Help! Help! Help!"

Around and under him surged and fought the entire pack.

The ladies screamed.

Men shouted.

The young men bolted out and over the inflowing stream of canines.

Two minutes later the pack and the preacher had undisputed possession of the Bungaree mission.

Then some of the young men rushed in with their stock whips, drove out the dogs and carried the curate in a half faint out into the open and tenderly deposited him on the grass.

Horses were mounted and the congregation suddenly dispersed. Fred and his brother assisted the curate into a dog cart and he was conveyed to the station, where he immediately took to his bed. The next morning he abandoned the mission. Squire White was indignant that such an outrage should have been committed and that his fox hounds should have led the procession.

Tom Moffatt, the White brothers and I after returning from church went out for a walk. We felt that our health demanded a walk beyond the hearing of the Squire.

If I remember aright, there was some laughter, but possibly I am mistaken.

"How was it done?"

"Why did they all want to get at the curate?"

"Where did they all come from?"

"Who originated the idea?"

"I think it must have happened in this way," answered Fred, "but you will all understand that it is a mere supposition."

"Our fox hounds were imported for the purpose of establishing a regular English hunt club in this district, other squatters intending to add to the pack. To exercise the dogs it is our custom to give them a weekly run and, to prevent them acquiring the habit of running kangaroos, we send a groom ahead on horseback dragging behind a red herring. On this trail the dogs run. This morning I fear that some person, not having the welfare of the mission at heart, must have set out at an early hour dragging a red herring, which they finally deposited in the pulpit at the chapel."

"But that does not account for the presence of all the other dogs in the country and the young men for twenty miles around, to say nothing about the escape of the hounds at an hour which enabled them to arrive when services were being conducted," remarked Moffatt.

"It is the unexpected which always happens," was Fred's answer.

On Monday, Moffatt and I returned to Adelaide, where I completed some business arrangements.

Fred White, who conducted a wool broking business at Port Adelaide, called upon us one afternoon and informed us that he was billed to appear that evening at a public meeting at the Port. A German, one of his best customers, was a candidate for a seat in the town council to fill a vacancy and had insisted upon Fred acting as chairman. Would we support him and grace the platform with our presence.

"Most assuredly," was the reply.

At eight o'clock that evening we filed into the hall at the Port, escorted by the chairman, who provided us with seats of honor.

The audience was decidedly mixed, half English, half German. The refreshments consisted of an unlimited supply of shandygaff.

When Fred attempted to call the meeting to order he was received with vociferous cheers, cat calls, applause and groans.

"Gentlemen," he began.

"Where are they?" shouted a voice.

"Citizens of Port Adelaide, we have met," continued Fred.

"What have we met?"

"Have a little patience," said Fred, with rising inflection.

"He's shouting patience. Shout beer and we are with you."

"I am a young man," said the chairman, fast losing his temper.

"A joey kangaroo," suggested a man on the front bench.

"You are a pretty bird," exclaimed Fred, pointing at the obnoxious individual.

"A laughing jackass from Bungaree," yelled the precocious small boy.

Fred abandoned his opening speech in disgust and introduced the candidate, a large, red-faced German, who soon convinced the rabble that he was there to stay. His speech pleased me exceedingly. It was as follows:

"Mr. chairman und beoples und vellow electors, I vas a vell known character mit dis constituency und otherwise. Ven I virst come to dis place vare vas now the Port it vas a vilderness vull of kangarooes und ouder kinds of beoples. I haf de honor of being de virst white man vat comes mit de down, mit de ocception of some ouder vellows vat comes in ahead of me. I haf de honor of building de virst house vat vas built in de down mit the occeptions of them ouder vellows vot comes in und builds up on de other zide of de street before I gets here yet already. Vats de matter?

"Ven I virst comes mit dis down dare vas den und schnide machinery mans going around mit his bogus machineries made out of gast iron, pot metal und shee oak und zelling dem to de varming gommunity beoples und beating dem out of der monies.

"I hunts arount und I vinds a vellow dat has vive douzand pounds gapital und I joins de ogsperience vot I got und dot gapital und ve vent to vork und built a voundry. Vot begomes of dot outside machinery mans? He vas shut out und ve done dot same kind of pezness ourselves.

"In less don vive years I got dot voundry, dot machineries, dot gapital, dot everyding. Dot ouder vellow don't got onydings, he vas no good already.

"You all knows vot drouble dot Black Creek has been mid de down. Der vas de varming peoples going in and getting der tings all vet and getting drownded. Who vas de means of de virst bridge agrost dat creek. I vas I, Samuel Muller, Esq. I vent to work mid the shire Gouncils und I vorked night und day, veek day und Sunday und every ouder times until I got the goncent of der gouncils to build dot bridge. Everbodys say, dat vas Sam Muller, he vas de instigator of dot bridge.

"Ven de next spring flood comes along avay goes dot bridge. Gentlemens, I have been de means und instigations of getting over a dozen bridges builded over dot creek und every von of dem vent avay. But hold on, vats de matter? After a vile I hear of iron bridge dot vas built of dot ouder place, Melbourne. Den I again vent to vork mid dose gouncils und vorks night und day und leaves no stones turned over undil I gets de goncent of der gouncils to build dot bridge.

"Ask dot leetle Sunday-school scholar dot vas going avay from Sunday-school mid his arms full of prizes, or dot dinner pail vot vas going along mid de school house, who vas de superintendent of dot bridge. Vot dey dolds you? Samuel Muller of de Port, he vas de archtecture.

"Yes, gentlemens, I build a great big stone butment on von side, und a great big stone one on de ouder side, und build de approages avay back level mid de town, und I baints ze bridge red.

"De next spring along gomes de flood, und de water back up mid dem approages, und vills up de zellars, vashes out de vollun vactory, de blaining mill, de vood yard, de lumber yard, de big pens und den all vent down de creek; but gentlemen, dot bridge stays. Dot vas de only ting dat did stay mid de down. Brovidence vas not zatisfied zo he gomes along mid Zeptember, mid more big floods, und avay goes dot bridge, likewise. He only goes down half a mile (de bridge not Brovidence), und we get him back again ready for de next flood.

"Dot ouder vellow dat vas running against me vos no good. He vas mid business in de down nine years ago und he vailed. He don't got a farthing.

"Seven years ago ven I vailed I gots more moneys dan ven I vas in business yet already.

"Und how vas it ven I back dat man's notes in Adelaide, und down gomes de bailiff and makes a jump on my broberty

"Dot vos an ice cream day.

"I don't got any broberty.

"Mrs. Sam owns it all.

PLUM HOLLOW. 187

"Vot vas de matter?"

"Gentlemans, you know de old saw, 'Zend a tief to catch a tief.'

"Gentlemans, you elect me on dot grounds und I catch dem all.

"You all know dat I haf not only zit in your gouncil chambers for two years, but I zit for three years in de Parliament at Adelaide, und as schure as der vas a Gott in Himmel I would haf dat ouder three years, only de ouder vellow dot vas against me got more votes vot I did.

"Now, gentlemens, you can't be too gareful who you elect to represent you mid de gouncil. You vant to zend a man dot has got a record for beating beoples, und on dot, gentlemans, I stand out und challenge de world und Port Adelaide. You vant to zend a man dot has got a parliament education und a municipal educations, und you know I have zit in Parliament three years, I have zit in your gouncil chamber two years, und mit de goncent of de beople I will go back vor de zird."

Long before the speech terminated the chairman, Tom Moffatt and I were laughing until the tears coursed down our cheeks.

Subsequently I saw in the Adelaide *Register* that Samuel Muller had been triumphantly returned at the head of the poll.

The following week Moffatt and I proceeded to Melbourne. We arrived the night before the Melbourne Cup was run. The race is the most important south of the line.

Here lies a great city of half a million people, where fifty years ago was only a solitary wattle and dab hut.

Through the city flows the Yarra Yarra river.

Out there, five miles away, lie Sandridge and Williamstown on Hobson's Bay.

Spanning the Yarra Yarra is Prince's Bridge, built at the cost of a million pound sterling. Upon the hill, the Law Courts, ranking among the most magnificent in the world; the University, with its beautiful chapel; the Trades' Hall, the Workingman's College, the Parliament Buildings and the Botanical Gardens, all tell the story of marvelous Melbourne.

From early morn a vast concourse of people are *en route* for Flemington, where the race is to be run.

Business is completely suspended.

Spencer Street railway station is a struggling mass of humanity. Out of the station, every five minutes, a train departs, carrying the eager, anxious throng.

We secure a seat.

The cares of life have vanished. Bank stocks, the fate of empires, politics, intrigue, love, law, all forgotten.

The horse reigns supreme.

Out of the car window we see the carriage road choked with humanity. Every color of the rainbow in flags and ribbons and dresses.

All pressing on to Flemington.

What a motley gathering!

The four-in-hand drag of the Governor-General, the costermonger's cart drawn by a patient donkey, women on foot, babies in arms, babies trying to walk, babies in perambulators, sleek, well-clothed Jews, rubicund publicans, vendors of native fruits, popping of champagne corks, hampers of luxuries, scant lunches folded in yesterday's newspapers, cripples hobbling forward, chaff, repartee, badinage and song.

All the world going to the Cup.

All the world out for a holiday.

Here we are!

The guard opens the door.

Down through the turnstiles.

This is Flemington.

Once seen, never forgotten.

A great amphitheatre.

To the right, the Saltwater river.

To the south, the Yarra Yarra.

Beyond, the great southern city.

Behind, stretching in an immense semi-circle, a cordon of hills, rising at an angle of forty-five degrees from the plain at your feet.

Nature made a race-course at Flemington.

Millions have been expended here, not only to fashion the finest race-course in the world, but to beautify and adorn, to furnish every comfort and convenience.

Paddocks and shelters for the fleet-footed horses.

Grand-stands, stretching for a quarter of a mile, rising terrace above terrace upon the hillside; restaurants and reception chambers, retiring rooms, telegraph offices, ambulance department with surgeons ready in case of accidents, fruit and flower stands. The course, a magnificent belt of emerald green, running in a straight line for seven furlongs and then sweeping in a great ellipse for two miles, and wide enough at the upper end for fifty horses to start abreast.

Remember, not a dusty, black track, but a beautiful

turf, smooth, elastic, fresh and sweet, waiting to be trodden by hoof-beats singing a song of motion.

Over there, the great ships lie sleeping and nodding in the harbor, dreaming of the storms gone by.

Above, an arch of cloudless blue, with the sun a ball of fire, slowly sinking in the west.

Here, at our feet, a green lawn, with fountains and flowers and music, and laughter and song.

Southern beauty resplendent in diamonds and silks and laces, full of grace and witchery.

Arched bands of flowers, with flamingo-colored blossoms drooping in great masses over little pools of bubbling waters.

This is Flemington.

A hoarse murmur, like the surf upon the distant shore, salutes you. It issues from a hundred thousand throats, and still they come to swell the throng.

Look over the flat (that is the space inside the course). Fifty thousand people have wedged themselves into a narrow belt directly opposite the grand stand and as near the winning post as possible.

Approach this motley throng. A hoarse roar rises and falls. Hundreds of bookmakers clothed in every fantastic and outlandish garment human ingenuity can devise. Some clad in blue silk jackets, with crimson trousers, and surmounted by paper hats three feet high. Fags and banners waving—everything to catch the eye. All shouting the odds on the horses. These are the cash bookies, who will wager you a tanner, a bob or a quid (slang terms for sixpence, a shilling or a sovereign). The but of every wag, they keep up a running fire of comment upon their tormentors, and at the same time do a roaring trade.

Where did all these people come from?

There are earls and barons and knights and ladies of high degree from "Merrie Old England," who have seen the Oaks, Doncaster and the Derby.

There are Frenchmen with waxed moustaches from Paris, Marseilles and Toulon who have cheered the winner of the Grand Prix.

There are Yankees with the New England accent from Boston; sharp-eyed bankers and brokers from New York, hoosiers with broad-brimmed sombreros from away out west, and millionaires from California.

There are Maoris from New Zealand, the land of the fleet-footed Moa and the still fleeter favorite, Trident. There are shepherds from the Barcoo in Queensland and the sand plains of Western Australia.

There are miners from the tin fields of Tasmania, from the gold fields of Ballarat, from the diamond fields of Bungaree and the opal bands of Queensland.

Enter the saddling paddock. Here are congregated the leviathan bookmakers of the southern hemisphere, and the horses which are to struggle for the cup.

The bell rings.

The saddles are strapped on, the jockeys weighed and mounted. One by one they file down the narrow pathway and out upon the course. Some of the horses sedate and anxious-eyed, as if mindful of the ten thousand sovereigns staked upon them. Some head-strong and restless, bolting down the course despite the little jocks who pull in vain.

Thirty horses gather in a wavering line up the strait.

One hundred and forty thousand people are watching every movement. For the first time to-day the bookmakers are silent.

Involuntarily every person in that vast concourse rises to his feet: twenty thousand field glasses are levelled upon Watson, the starter.

At first little murmurs break from the spectators. They are but spasmodic.

Then comes the cry, "They're off!"

Not another word is uttered.

Every lip, which at the start was open, is now firm shut.

You can almost hear the beating of one hundred and forty thousand hearts.

The thin line of horses with their riders glittering in the distinctive colors of their stables wavers for a few brief seconds, as if a gigantic colored snake were slowly coiling itself up and then suddenly breaks. You see the sunlight flash through the rifts and openings in the line. Behind, a little cloud of dust rolls over the green turf and rapidly sinks to rest.

With straining eyes and bated breath you lean forward: every second seems an age. Then the horses and riders flash out distinctly. The blue, the green and gold, the crimson, the yellow and black, the orange with silver bars. You know them all.

In the front rank ten noble horses true as steel.

In the second rank another ten.

Behind, a dozen in the mob.

You hear the crisp grass snap beneath their flying feet.

Ere the heart can beat again they are gone.

A good two miles are yet before them. Then, for the first time since they started, you draw a long breath.

Where is the favorite, Trident?

In the mob, running with head low, skimming the ground like a greyhound.

Ha! Out of the second rank, as they turn the half-mile post, a beautiful black horse sweeps to the fore, struggles for a brief instant with the scarlet colors, which so far have led the van, then forges to the front.

Another change: the orange with silver bars has shot his bolt and falls behind into the mob.

Aha! There is a gleam of green and gold flashing in the sunlight. Bolt upright sits the rider, there is but one such in the Southern world—Tom Hales. Trident is in the second line.

Down the great ellipse they all come flying at a mighty pace. They reach the last turn, Silvermine a good two lengths ahead with half a dozen at his heels. Next the green and gold swinging along with Hales' boot grazing the rail.

What a sight!

The colors gleaming in the sunlight. One hundred and forty thousand people spellbound, entranced.

Not a sound comes up from that vast multitude.

Not a whisper falls upon the air.

How they are riding!

Out of the ellipse?

Yes.

Into the home stretch.

One, two, three, four, five horses.

Which will win?

Oh!

Silvermine has it.

Through a narrow gap between two horses a head shoots out. Again you catch the gleam of green and gold.

Like a shaft shot from a yew tree bow the New Zealand horse springs forward.

You hear the hoof-beats.

With nostrils distended Silvermine leaps out with redoubled fury.

Horse and rider merge into a single mass of velocity.

Now they are side by side.

Ten jumps will tell the story.

Hales rises in his saddle.

Trident, as if spurred by an electric shock, makes one superhuman effort and shoots under the wire a neck ahead.

You have seen the Melbourne Cup.

Leaving Melbourne we proceeded to Sydney and secured our passage on the Orient liner, "Orizaba," *en route* for England. The six weeks' run was without incident. From Moffatt I gleaned a few facts that threw some light upon his past life and the causes which induced him to bury himself in the solitude of the Australian desert.

He was the only child of Sir John Moffatt, a retired East India officer, who had won his title for bravery during the Sepoy Mutiny. On leaving the service Sir John had retired to an extensive estate on the Straits of Dover. Tom, at the age of twenty, met his fate in the person of a beautiful girl of Italian descent, though born in England. Some mystery hung about the family, which consisted of an only brother and sister. It was whispered by envious tongues that the dark beauty had a strain of African blood in her veins, and this coming to the ears of Sir John simultaneously with Tom's announcement that he had proposed and been accepted, led to a stormy scene between father and son. Sir John's pride was based upon the purity of the Moffatt blood. That an heir to his name and estates should be born at whom the finger of scorn could be pointed, was more than he could bear. He loved his son devotedly, but this only served to make his anger the hotter.

Tom rushed up to London and married the girl. As he possessed a small annuity, a legacy from his deceased mother, the young couple succeeded for a time in living in a moderate way; but such a life was ill-suited to the luxurious tastes and ambition of the bride, who humiliated herself by writing to Sir John and begging forgiveness, only to have her letter returned. Then she more than hinted to her husband that she had been trapped and deceived. To reduce expenses Tom removed from London to Chester, where he obtained an agency from a mercantile firm which necessitated his travelling a portion of his time.

Despite her folly and her temper Tom loved his wife with an ardour rendering him blind to her faults. When a little girl was born to them his heart went out to the child with a fondness intense in its devotion. For a time his wife entertained hopes that Sir John would relent, but when no sign came she threw off all restraint and upbraided her husband with having inveigled her into marriage under false pretences. This charge, so false, exasperated him and widened the estrangement. The fonder the father became of the child the less affection was bestowed upon it by the mother. Yet Tom entertained the hope that in the end all would be well.

On his return after a week's absence he found that his wife had abandoned him and the child, leaving behind a note stating that it would be useless to attempt to trace her, as she had left England forever. Every means were exhausted to discover her hiding-place, but in vain. Her brother refused to interest himself in the search.

Securing a home for the child with a distant relative, Tom sailed for Australia and soon drifted into the desert, preferring its solitude to the companionship of men. The White family had known his father in early days, learning of his presence in Adelaide, had come to him in a friendly way, taken him up to their station, but were powerless in preventing him from burying himself in the back blocks.

My appearance at the telegraph station had awakened in him a desire for companionship, which he found must be gratified. A letter from his father, urging him to return, and his love for his child had caused him to go back to England.

On our arrival in London, Moffatt made me promise that I would run down to Moffatt Manor and pay him a long visit, when I had attended to my financial affairs in Lombard Street. A few days later I received a letter, in which he stated that his reconciliation with his father had been complete, that his child was with them and that Sir John had already grown very fond of her.

Jagga Jagga and I were weary of the great city.

One sunny morning we took the train at Charing Cross and were soon flying through the green lanes of England. At the manor house our welcome was enthusiastic. Sir John, a stately gentleman of seventy, with the courtly grace of the past century and the hospitality of an Englishman, and Tom Moffatt, with his breezy freshness, made a charming pair, the picture being completed by the little daughter, Hazel, clinging to her father's hand.

From the first Hazel took with childish fancy to Jagga Jagga, calling him "Black-em-man." She gave him her heart without reserve and made him her slave for all time to come. The days passed very pleasantly, but I soon discovered that Tom's passionate love for his child was almost abnormal in its intensity. All the old love for the mother, which five years in the desert had not completely blotted out, came back and centred upon Hazel, whose artless innocence was irresistible to men long removed from the prattle of childhood. When Jagga Jagga threw his boomerang her merry laughter made the leaves on the great oak, under which we sat, rustle with ripples of delight.

In two weeks I had grown to look upon the manor house as my English home and my departure was indefinitely postponed.

One pleasant morning Tom was called away to the county town upon business. Jagga Jagga and Hazel were out in the copse to see the robins' nest and the young robins just come to robindom. Sir John was writing in the library. I decided upon a stroll through the wood. My ramble led me along the coast and extended so far that I determined to forego tiffin. Some three miles from the manor house was a precepitous cliff, covered with tangled underwood, but crowned near the edge with a gigantic oak, often admired by me from a distance. A zig-zag path ran out to the shelving rock overhanging the sea nearly one hundred feet below. I entered the path and forced my way through the tangled foliage. Suddenly there rang out a cry of despair from the shelving rock, not fifty yards distant, but hidden by the thick leaves. I sprang forward to the opening, but no person was visible. A small canvas bag lay on the rock, over the edge of which I peeped, where I saw, lying on a projection a few feet above the water, the form of a man, who must have fallen over the precipice but a few seconds before. I could hear men shouting further down the coast, but they were not visible. I started back in horror, and, in doing so, struck my foot against the canvas bag, which clinking told me that it contained gold. Mechanically I took it up and started running parallel with the cliff, in the hope of finding some place to descend to the injured man. I soon came upon a rude path constantly descending diagonally along the cliff. Down this incline I plunged, regardless of slipping and falling stones following in my track. When but a few feet from the sea I found myself in a *cul du sac*. The path suddenly stopped before a pile of huge and irregular rocks. As I stood there panting for breath a man close at hand and evidently in a boat beneath me shouted, "Hold on! Hold on!"

The next moment I was in the grasp of two powerful men, who had clambered up the rocks. I was thrown to the ground with a violence which nearly deprived me of my senses. My elbows were then bound together by a stout cord, and I was pulled and pushed down and into the boat. Recovering my senses I cried out, "A man has fallen over the cliff; go to his assistance; he may not be dead."

"Yes, you villian, we knew all about the man," was the response of the fellow who still grasped me by the collar.

"You inhuman brutes," I gasped, "Why don't you go to him. If you want to rob me you can do so later on." For I was convinced that I had fallen into the hands of thieves.

"Inhuman brutes," repeated the man. "You are a cool un, you be," and then he shook me violently.

"I will give you a hundred pounds if you will go to the assistance of the unfortunate man," I exclaimed.

"And pay us with his own money," answered the fellow at the oars, pointing to the canvas bag.

"Perhaps he is not dead," said my custodian to his companion.

"Fell a hundred feet plump on the rocks and dead as a door nail," was the answer.

Then he pulled away to a point just underneath where the man had fallen. Fastening the boat, he climbed up and shouted back, "Dead!"

"Do you know him?"

"Yes."

"Who?"

"Sir John Moffatt, as I'm a living man!"

"It cannot be," I cried, springing to my feet. "I left him writing in the library at the manor house.

"Throw me a rope," came from above.

The rope was thrown.

Ten minutes after the mangled remains dangled over the edge of the rock and soon rested in the bow of the boat.

"Poor Sir John," I moaned. "What a frightful accident. How could it have happened? It will break Tom's heart."

The men spoke not a word.

"What a frightful accident," I moaned.

"Don't you call it an accident again or I'll hang you myself," my captor exclaimed.

This threat startled me. Could it be that these wretches had murdered my dear friend and intended to charge me with the crime?

We proceeded down the coast half a mile, where a fishing hamlet nestled in a little harbor. Outside the harbor a steam yacht was lying with steam up and her ladder down ready for passengers. At the opening of the rift in the coast line we met a boat pulled by four stout men, with two passengers, both ladies. They swept by, pulling at a rapid rate in the direction of the yacht, and had proceeded but a short distance when a young woman, with a great mass of tawny hair, sprang with a scream into the sea. The tide, which was running in, swept her in our direction, and ere the other boat could be brought up she drifted and swam to our craft and was pulled aboard. The other boat came back and a tall man with a dark complexion stood up and commanded my companions to return her to his craft.

"I will not go," said the rescued woman stoutly, "and I claim your protection from a villian."

My companions hesitated for a moment, when one

of them said to the stranger, "If this lady does not want to go on board the yacht, then she goes ashore with us."

At this instant the stranger caught sight of the lifeless remains of Sir John in the bow of the boat. He turned deadly pale, whispered hurriedly to the woman beside him, and the next instant they were pulling away for the yacht.

Five minutes after we landed at the cove, and in the confusion which followed I lost sight of the rescued woman.

The entire population of the hamlet soon surrounded us. "Murder! Murder!" was whispered with quivering lips. The looks which met me brought conviction that I was branded as the perpetrator of the crime. A dog cart was secured, and two hours after I found myself in the strongest cell of the county jail, charged with the murder of Sir John Moffatt. The only information I secured from the turnkey was that the coroner's inquest would be held the next day

The following morning I obtained permission to secure counsel, and, on the advice of the jailer, summoned Mr. Webster, the leading barrister of the town, to whom I related all the circumstances. A hurried note containing the facts was despatched to Tom Moffatt and preparations made for attending the coroner's inquest, held at the fishing hamlet, where I was escorted by a strong guard.

My arrival was greeted with hisses and cries of "Pitch him into the sea." In the midst of this scene

Tom Moffatt came forward and confronting me said, "Martyne! Guilty or innocent?"

"Innocent."

Then he held out both of his hands and grasped mine, while the tears ran down his cheeks, as he sobbed, "My poor, old father! My poor, old father! Gone, gone, and my best friend charged with his murder."

The jury was empanelled, the court organized and the examination begun.

The first witness was William Poole, whom I recognized as one of my captors. His testimony was as follows:—

"I am in the coast guard service, have been a member of the force for twenty years. Knew Sir John Moffatt. Yesterday, in company with James Rowland, another guard, we were in a boat concealed under some bushes on the coast, a short distance from the great oak on the shelving rock. Our suspicions of smugglers had been aroused by the appearance of a steam yacht which hovered about the coast. From where we were we could distinctly see the shelving rock, on which the great oak stands, though the distance was too great to recognize a man's features distinctly. Naturally our eyes were on the yacht and not the shore. At about half-past three I heard a shout, followed by cries on the shelving rock. Looking up, I saw two men struggling. One was an old man with white hair, his back was toward the sea; the other man was not so tall, and, being behind the first man, I could not see his face. The struggle only lasted a brief space of time, when the old man was pushed over the precipice and fell nearly one hundred feet to the rocks below. Just as the man fell my companion and I shouted and instantly the murderer disappeared in the brushwood behind the oak. We started to row in that direction when the man reappeared, looked over the cliff where Sir John lay, picked up something from the rock, and ran rapidly down the cliff in the direction opposite to us. I knew the path he had taken terminated near the water's edge. From the time he left the shelving rock until we made him a prisoner he was never out of our sight."

The coroner inquired, "Would you recognize the man?"

"Certainly," Poole answered. "There he stands," pointing to me.

"Did you find anything with the prisoner?"

"Yes; a canvas bag, containing two hundred sovereigns."

The bag was produced. Written on the top in a large bold hand was the name, "Sir John Moffatt."

The next witness was James Rowland, Poole's companion, and also a coast guard. His evidence was substantially the same as Poole's.

Mr. Webster, in his cross-examination, failed to shake the testimony in the slightest particular, and I was committed to stand my trial for the murder of Sir John Moffatt.

The court would meet in about four weeks and Mr. Webster informed me that unless we secured new evidence throwing light upon the case it would be wise to have the case postponed until the assizes, to be held four months later, as I had everything to gain by the delay. This proposal I rejected; firm in my innocence I could not consent to languish in jail.

A dectective from Scotland Yard was secured and every effort put forth by Mr. Webster and Tom Moffatt to obtain a clue, but in vain. Suspicion at first pointed to the mysterious yacht, but it was soon ascertained that the yacht belonged to a wealthy London gentleman. The young lady who had jumped overboard from the small boat had left the hamlet the same evening, no attention having been paid to her during the confusion incidental to my arrival and departure to the county jail.

The only hope held out by Mr. Webster was that the jury would disagree, owing to Tom Moffatt's staunch belief in my innocence and the fact that the perpetrator of the crime had never been seen distinctly by the principal witnesses. The defence being that I had accidently appeared on the scene immediately after his disappearance in the brushwood. Of course it would be shown that the paltry two hundred pounds would be no temptation to a man in my financial position.

From Tom Moffatt I learned that Jagga Jagga had mysteriously disappeared upon learning of the death of Sir John and that I had been sent to prison. My heart bled for the poor fellow and I gave orders that the most diligent search should be made for him.

BOOK V.

A STRUGGLE FOR FAME.

With the inspiration, derived from the contemplation of great paintings, there came to Rue the desire to portray her conception of the beautiful. Her efforts were signal failures. They lacked the originality and force so manifest in her earlier productions. They were no longer nature interpreted by Rue Jahns, but feeble imitations of other works. She knew that success could only be achieved by loyalty to her own convictions. To paint a great picture is to embody our own conceptions in color, for no two persons voice sentiments of the same import. She strove in vain to shake off her besetting sin. Then she laid aside her brushes and waited. A great impulse might arouse her to redoubled efforts, without which her dreams would dissolve into thin air. The crisis was full of poignant disappointment, and there were hours when she felt that her ambition was but the fancies of a child—a dreaming girl. Yet such was the strength of her will that she was not wholly given over to despair. Sunlit days, when the hopes of the Point flushed her heart with exquisite fancies, shifting and intangible, but brimful of blessings.

She wandered from gallery to gallery, catching from mantles of the past glimpses of the immortal. Every line of beauty spoke in trumpet tones, every combination of color was a poem, every grace of pose a revelation; not in lines of beauty, or blended colors, or grace of pose did she find her chief delight, but in the painter's ideal. In battle scenes she heard the roar of the cannon, the rattle of the musketry, the clank of the sabre, the tramp of the squadrons, the galloping of the cavalry, the moans of the dying and the shouts of victory.

In pastoral delineations the sweet fresh air of spring, the sultry sleepy heat of summer, the purple tints of autumn and the icy blasts of winter were lived over again. The dim and shadowy banks of the Nile, springing from their desert of sand, with the Pharoahs in their tombs, and the falaheen of the mud hut, the swarthy Nubian and the fierce Dervish, the Bedowin and the cry, "Allah, il Allah," flitted before her—a majestic panorama—in the Egyptian pictures.

The stately court of Louis XIV., with its courtiers and beautiful women, its magnificence and its follies, swept by as she stood beside the mute but eloquent canvas and drank in inspiration.

Amid all these momentoes of the past, these priceless heirlooms, eloquent in chanting rythms of feeling, there were times when she grew very sad. Themes so vast in import, so pregnant with thought, flitted through her brain and beckoned her forward. She saw the sons and daughters of La Belle France landing at Tadousac, the founding of Villa Marie, the priests paddling up the St. Lawrence and the Ottawa, over the great lakes and down to the Father of Waters,

> "Whose long arms o'er the prairies tossed,
>   With feet that bathed in tropic spray."

She felt that the hour had struck when a daughter of the Great North Land should repay the debt of gratitude.

Nearly a year had gone by since her arrival in Paris when, finding that her studies were to her barren of results, she determined to visit Italy.

Coming out of Notre Dame one afternoon she suddenly found herself face to face with Majeroni, who stood admiring the flying buttresses of the cathedral.

"You in Paris," he exclaimed. "When did you arrive? I need not ask your mission. Beloved art. Art the loadstone, and Canada's daughter responds."

His was the first face linked with her home she had looked upon since leaving La Rue's Mills.

"I have been here some months," Rue said, extending her hand.

"You left no trail behind you when you so suddenly disappeared," remarked Majeroni.

Then they chatted of the river she loved so well.

Rue said "Good bye," and turned to go.

"Not good bye, Miss Jahns," Majeroni exclaimed. "Surely I shall meet you again, for my stay in Paris will not be short. I have never paid my debt of gratitude to you for having saved my life, and, as I know the city well, there must be places of interest—private galleries—which, with an escort, you would wish to visit. My very poor services are entirely at your disposal. It would afford me the greatest pleasure to be of some service."

The offer was so cordial and the desire to please so apparent that Rue relented. It was then understood that they were to meet the following day at the Louvre.

The meeting was made pleasant by a stroll through the galleries, in which the great masterpieces were admired and criticised by Majeroni in his half cynical way.

As they strolled along the boulevard Majeroni inquired, "Are you content to feast your eyes on canvas to the exclusion of humanity?"

"No, far from it," Rue answered. "One must study nature as well as canvas. For years I only studied nature on the banks of the dear old river. In Paris I study humanity as well as the art of producing effects."

"In studying humanity you must analyze character," continued Majeroni. "What are your conclusions?'

"Oh! I have not arrived at conclusions, they are yet a long way off. I am but a young traveller just set out on that road."

"What has been the result of all your months of study?"

"At first I began studying the dress of the people, not the fashion plates that promenade the boulevards, but the men and women, and even the little children. I am a child of the people myself. I soon grew to study the faces as types of character."

"To which class have you relegated me," Majeroni inquired.

"Not yet classified," Rue answered.

"Don't include me with the puzzle variety."

"I'm inclined to do so. But, seriously, something is very wrong."

"Again I am in the dark."

"I cannot make it plain as I have never spoken of it before. Perhaps you can help me if I tell you what I feel. Poverty and misery, misery and poverty is the refrain whispered over this great city. Why? I inquire again and again. The only answer given is 'drink and ignorance.' But why drink and ignorance? Why poverty, also with frugality? Why want with all the virtues of temperance, honesty and thrift? Why toil when there should be rest? Can you give me the answer?"

"I can only say relieve with charity," he answered.

"I hate that word charity," said Rue, her eyes flashing. "The people hate it, too; they don't want it; they want opportunity, that is work, and pay for their work. They want land on which to build homes. They are land hungry."

"They cannot satisfy their land hunger without money, unless they rob owners of their property," Majeroni answered, "and you certainly do not believe in peculation."

"Who gave the land to the people?"

"The Creator."

"Did He give it to the few or to all?"

"To all, certainly."

"Then why do the few claim it to the exclusion of the many?"

"That is the problem of the survival of the fittest."

"Is such a conclusion Christ-like?"

"At any rate it is a fact."

"Who decides as to the fittest?"

"Really, Miss Jahns, you are becoming a Socialist, or, even worse, an Anarchist. Where did you imbibe such revolutionary ideas?"

"I know nothing of Socialists or Anarchists; but I do know of misery and poverty, and struggles and despair, and I feel that behind it all there is a great wrong, and for that wrong there must be a cure. I believe that it is a man-made curse, the infinite Father could not have been the author; and that curse concerns me, you—all mankind. What is the remedy?"

"Education and the church," suggested Majeroni.

"Education and the church be hanged," retorted the impetuous girl. "But, seriously, you can't educate the mental or stimulate the moral faculties of a hungry man. The people must have bread and homes first, then the others will follow."

"Do you advise war?"

"No. I want peace. I want the people to think; but, poor creatures, they have no time for thought and some one must point out the way. Then there will arise an army of willing helpers from the middle classes and the church must come to their assistance or die. Once the light is visible it may flicker and fade and wane, but the breath of truth will keep it alive until it bursts into a glorious flame."

Majeroni listened with astonishment to what he regarded as the rhapsody of a young and impetuous girl. He knew that her whole soul was burning with enthusiasm and melting with pity, and his knowledge of her force of character warned him not to trample upon any of her cherished opinions. He felt he had established the first bond of mutual confidence.

From that day, for two months, their meetings were frequent in the galleries. After a time Majeroni suggested to Rue a visit to parts of the city never frequented by her, where pictures of note could be seen in old churches and private galleries, to which he easily obtained access. Then he suggested an evening at the opera or the theatre. Rue had never seen a play and finally consented to see the divine Sara in Cleopatra. From the arrival of the royal barge until the tragic death of the Egyptian queen, Rue sat as one in a trance. The melting melody of Sara's liquid voice wove about her a spell from which she did not recover until she found herself in the open air. Majeroni had watched her narrowly during the performance and had not disturbed her reverie by even a casual remark.

"What did you think of the play?" he inquired, as they stood on the pavement.

What a wonderful woman!" Rue said. "I never thought that a human voice could coo like a bird, whisper like a leaf, sigh like the rain, or moan like the pines. A wonderful, wonderful woman. She feels it all. She is indeed Cleopatra. Give me her spirit and I will paint a glorious picture. How poor and weak and halting have I been, but she has taught me a lesson."

When she bade Majeroni good night, she said, "You have been very kind. I am going away from Paris. I have no more time to squander."

The next day she left for Rome, leaving no clue behind her by which she could be traced. Rue's sudden departure arose from a variety of causes. Her money was melting away, her lessons in drawing had proved a failure. Since her meeting with Majeroni her studies at the galleries had been far from satisfactory. She found herself drifting from a single purpose demanding all her energies. When in his presence she felt that by insensible degrees he was gradually acquiring an influence over her fatal to her cherished hopes, and yet she could not divest herself of the thought that he cared nothing for art or for her success but was actuated by a purpose which her success would frustrate.

Once in Rome, she secured a very humble apartment in the Jewish quarter, near the ruins of the Forum.

The change from gay Paris to crumbling Rome produced a startling effect upon her. The ancient city flung wide a new avenue into which she entered. It was the Past, written in grey stone and sculptured in polished marble, in fluted capitals and statues, in crumbling wall and Gothic chambers, in triumphal arch and mosaic pavement. She revelled in these new-found pleasures, and Baedker in hand, trod the historic ground with reverent footsteps. She experienced no desire to visit the picture galleries; a hunger for knowledge was upon her.

In her wanderings she strolled into the Collegio Romano to consult a book in the Biblioteca Vittoria Emanuele. By accident she came upon the translation of the "Jesuit Relations," published by the Canadian government. Instantly all the ardour, fanned into a flame by Parkman's book, was rekindled with redoubled intensity. She read until twilight warned her the day was gone and that she was very hungry. For weeks she haunted the library until she finished the last chapter of the last volume. Then she arose, full of strength, confidence, hope. In Canada the torch had been lighted in her young soul beside the blazing pine-knots in the cabin on the Point; in Rome it burst into a lambent flame. She felt that the consummation of her mission to the Eternal City was at hand. The Jesuit church of S. Ignazo adjoined the library and near at hand the

General of the Order resided. Sixty thousand volumes and two thousand MSS. from the old library of the order were within her reach. She decided to obtain an interview with the General of the Society, ask his advice and, if necessary, assistance. Her application was granted. Rue was not a Roman Catholic, but as a child she had imbibed many prejudices against the Society from which she could not divest herself. She felt that the highest dignitary might question her upon these points and in consequence refuse his assistance.

Her reception was hospitable and re-assuring, but she never understood how it happened that within half-an-hour she had given the General an epitome of her whole life while only intending to discuss the lives of the martyrs in Canada. In return she had not only been encouraged, but commanded to begin her work at once. To her had been assigned a sacred trust, to perpetuate the heroic martyrdom of the heralds of the Cross in the Great North Land. She was assured that all aids within the reach of the General would be placed at her disposal.

The cost of the canvas and paints required for her work nearly exhausted her savings, leaving her dependent upon the monthly remittance from Squire Mallory. The brave girl struggling under these difficulties, gave up every comfort and became content with mere existence. Before her mind's eye flitted, not one, but half a hundred subjects jostling each other for supremacy. Out of this chaos she made a selection and set to work. The superabundace of themes running riot in her brain prevented the accomplishment of any definite conception. Without the means to buy new canvas, she was compelled again and again to clean the old and make a new trial. Some of her attempts were of great promise, some crude, but all failures. Her technical skill lagged behind her imagination, clogging her footsteps, and bringing bitter tears of disappointment. She suffered as only genius can suffer. Glades of the Canadian forest crowded with Hurons and Iroquois surrounding the few fearless sons of the Church, appeared and re-appeared on her canvas in rapid confusion. The simple expanded into the prolix and then dwindled into the common-place. In this swirl of conflicting subjects she found no rest. Five months had gone by, her frame had shrunk, her eyes blazed with unnatural fires, her cheeks were hollow, and her hands trembled. As her physical strength declined the spirit within her drove her forward with redoubled fury. Could she have dispassionately examined the struggle, she would have perceived that every successive failure was a means to the end. A central truth ran through each attempt, now half-hidden, now bursting forth. This germ which she labored to imprison on canvas, was infinite pity appealing to humanity. Worn out and exhausted by the struggle, Rue sat with hands crossed; a pathetic smile lingered about her mouth as she looked down upon her last failure. The tears dimmed her eyes and hope sank in her breast. There was a sudden knock at the door, which quickly opened and Majeroni entered, exclaiming, "I have found you at last."

"Me?"

"Yes, you. For months I have searched in vain every picture gallery in Italy, for I felt that in this country you must have hidden."

"Why should you be seeking?"

"Because you ran away from me."

"Mr. Majeroni!"

"What have you been doing, why are you here in this garret? You are pale; you have been ill."

"No, only working very hard," said Rue with a sigh.

"This must not go on," exclaimed Majeroni with vehemence. You must abandon these insane attempts. With your talents success is assured under favorable conditions. You need wealth, luxury. I place them at your feet. Be mine and every wish shall be gratified. I have loved you from the first."

Rue turned deadly pale, but answered never a word.

"Do not decide against me," Majeroni whispered, with an intensity born of long pent-up passion.

"It can never be" Rue said with trembling lips.

"Why?"

"Because I cannot, do not love you. Forget the present and——"

"Never," broke in Majeroni, trembling with passion, forgetting all restraint, "I say you shall be mine, and no power on earth shall prevent it. Your painting is a failure."

He advanced with outstretched arms.

The old Jahns' spirit slumbering in her blood burst into a red flame. No Jahns had ever been a coward. With flashing eye she faced him and hissed out, "Begone you Italian dog."

He hesitated, paused, and then a smile crept over his face, as he left the room and passed slowly down the stairs. That smile never left his face. In the open air he hummed a bar of "Robert le Diable," and then murmured to himself; "Foiled, defeated, but not conquered. My pretty Jahns, I would have married you, now you shall feel the vengeance of an Italian dog. A trip on the Mediterrean might curb and break your haughty spirit. Ha! Ha!"

When Majeroni departed Rue sat with folded arms and tight-shut lips and gazed out upon the blue sky and distant mountain peaks, but she saw them not. Had she been a man she would have followed him and shot him without compunction. The threat which he had uttered could be scorned and forgotten, the taunt of her failure, never. For two consecutive days she brooded and again set to work. With her the die was cast. If failure came, it would be her last effort.

BOOK VI.

THE SALON.

The doors of the Paris Salon were opened.

Into the great corridors swept the beauty, wit, fashion and culture of the gay capital.

The walls blossomed with triumphs of the brush. Patient mediocrity, skill won by years of toil, daring conceptions striving for fame, masters of color and tone crowned with laurels of the past, audacious inexperience, conscious power waiting on the line or mounted skyward, impatient, anxious, trembling for the crucial test—the verdict of the people.

Catalogue in hand, the arbiters of the artists' destiny sauntered forward, smiling, chatting, bowing, pausing for a brief moment to admire and praise, or hurrying away from a condemned effort. The tide swept on, a placid stream, broken only by *bon mots* and laughter.

To the few a wedding march of triumph, for many disaster and defeat.

Suddenly the procession halts. The advance guard has stopped.

A murmur of dissent runs through the spectators.

A little bird whispers from ear to ear, "A great picture."

Impatience seizes upon the multitude.

The placid stream of humanity breaks into a turbulent wave and then into an angry sea.

The timid fall behind.

The strong press forward.

Away up the line you catch glimpses of a confused mass, in striking contrast with the eager, advancing host.

Heads are bowed in reverence, lips parted in admiration, devotees kneel in prayer, eyes long bleared by lust and hearts smitten with the palsy of avarice drop tears of pity and beat responsive to the touch of genius.

Down the corridors a name floats, unknown by all save one in that vast multitude. It is whispered from lip to lip until, bursting from the Salon in a volume of praise, it is caught up by the great city, runs across continents and under seas, dying away in the uttermost parts.

That name is Rue Jahns.

The painting—A wild waste of mountains in the background, clothed with pine and hemlock, the valley clad with spruce and balsam and overhung by the mists of a March day, into which drift great volumes of smoke. The first impression—desolation, a requiem of mournful solemnity, a vast canopy hiding a great crime. Draw nearer; faces, sardonic in ferocity, peep from the clouds of smoke and gleam upon you with distended eyes. Hell itself has sent its cohorts to gloat over a barbarous triumph. Another step forward, through a gap in the distant mountains streams a ray of light, piercing the shadows, then broadening until it falls upon the foreground. Reflected from this light and half revealed, is a Huron village, Saint Ignace. The ashes of burned lodges lie thick and black on the frozen ground with patches of snow, red with Indian blood. Half-consumed bodies thrust charred and bony fingers from the darkness. Here and there dead infants lay with faces upturned and eyes yet full of fear. Down the valley in headlong flight plunge a group of Hurons, closely pursued by half a score of Iroquois. The palisade, breached and broken, coils about the scene with snake-like convolutions. This revel of the imps grows upon you until the soul shudders with horror and hot blood cries out for vengeance. Then succeeds a great change, vengeance and hatred and anger die out and infinite pity bids you bow in reverent awe.

Bound to a stake with fagots slowly burning at his feet, a Jesuit priest, his tall form erect and defiant, no look of pain or agony, yet scorched from head to feet. On his neck a collar of hatchets, heated red hot, burning by slow degrees into a breast brave as ever covered human heart. Behind, a renegade Huron slowly pouring boiling water upon the bowed head of the martyr, from whom an Iriquois cuts strips of flesh, which the savages eagerly devour. To the right stands Lalemant, about his naked body strips of bark smeared with pitch, ignited by a fiend, as Lalemant utters the memorable words, "*We are made a spectacle to the world, to angels and to men.*"

At Brebouf's feet kneels a Huron woman, with face upturned, beceeching baptism. Brebouf's face is toward the suppliant. A smile wreaths his lips. We feel that his soul chants, "*Gloria in Excelcis.*" Infinite compassion sits upon his blackened brow as he calmly waits for death.

From this last sad scene the eye turns to the band of light streaming from the far-off mountain gap, now scintilating with a radience before unseen. Angels faces and forms cluster in its shining waves and beckon the martyr Home.

BOOK VII.

THE TRIAL.

The day of trial came.

The court-room packed to suffication.

I stood in the prisoner's box charged with murder and according to English law prevented from giving any testimony myself. Tom Moffatt never flinched in his loyalty to me and with Mr. Webster stood by my side when the indictment was read.

The trial went on; in all main particulars being a repetition of the investigation held by the coroner, save that Poole and Rowland were more positive as to my being the person who threw Sir John over the cliff. Time had strengthened this conviction, and thus I saw the chief ground for my hope slip from beneath me. The evidence for the defence consisted of the testimony of my London banker, showing the sum at my credit, and Tom Moffatt's statement in my behalf.

The barrister for the Crown arose to address the jury.

A court official thrust a note into Mr. Webster's hand.

Instantly he was on his feet.

"My Lord," he said, "I have another witness, and a very important one for the defence, to call; a witness of whose existence I was ignorant until this moment."

The Crown prosecutor protested against re-opening the case.

His Lordship ruled that the new witness must be heard.

A beautiful girl came forward.

The first glance told me she was the woman rescued from the sea by my captors on the day of the murder.

"Your name?" asked the clerk of the court, as he prepared to administer the oath.

A hush fell upon the multitude.

"Rue Jahns," was the answer.

My breath came with difficulty.

Rue Jahns, a witness in my defence.

I had parted with her a mere child, in a tattered dress, on the broken mill stone at La Rue's Mills in Canada. She stood before me a queenly woman in an English court-room.

Mr. Webster hesitated and then said, "Your name?"

"Rue Jahns."

"A native of England?"

"No; a Canadian."

"Your rank or position?"

"An artist."

"Did you ever see the prisoner before?"

"Yes; once in Canada and once in England."

"When in England?"

"The day of the death of Sir John Moffatt."

"Miss Jahns, will you state to the court what you know about this case?"

"On the day of the murder, in the afternoon, I was at Fishport (the little hamlet near the shelving rock). I went there with a lady who wished me to make a sketch of the coast for her. We were being taken in a small boat to a steam yacht, lying off the port, when I discovered that one of the occupants of the boat was a man whom I had reason to fear. I asked to be put on shore, but no attention was paid to my request. Then I jumped into the sea, and was rescued by these men (pointing to Poole and Rowland). Mr. Martyne was in the boat at the time, but I did not recognize him. It was not until we arrived at Fishport that I discovered that the boat also contained a corpse. During the excitement I made my way out of the hamlet and sat down in a sunny place until my clothes were partially dry. Enquiring for the nearest railway station, I was directed to Congo, ten miles distant, where I arrived after dark. At the hotel I was refused a room, owing, no doubt, to my appearance, but was advised to apply to Mrs. Fenshaw, a lady who resided on the outskirts of the town, and who let rooms to lodgers. To her I related my story and by her was received with kindness. The three following days I was ill and unable to leave my room. On the fourth evening I ventured out for a short walk and behind a hedge came suddenly upon a black man crouching on the ground. I was startled, but did not run away. Then the man came forward and, pointing to his mouth, said, in broken English, 'Eatem! Eatem!' I understood that he was hungry. Then I asked him to come with me to the cottage for food, but he refused. I told him I would bring him some, which I did. He devoured it, and then said, 'Master, master Martyne pay you.'

"'Carl Martyne?' I inquired.

"'Yes, Carlee Martyne, my master,' and the poor fellow burst into tears and sobbed like a child.

"'Must go,' he said. 'Eatem here when sun comes up,' and away he went, despite my entreaties for him to remain.

"Years before, a Carl Martyne had been very kind to me when I was a poor child in Canada. I had never forgotton him, and in this black man felt that I had discovered a clue to my benefactor, which I determined to follow. The next morning I was at the same place with food. At sunrise the black man came and was very friendly. His command of English was so limited that it was with great difficulty that I elicited the following facts, and only after I assured him that I knew his master and was his friend:—

"'Master was in great trouble, they had taken him away. Man dead. Master no kill man, love him very much. Somebody kill man, he (the black) find him, then kill him very much.'

"This imperfect story excited my curiosity and sympathy, and an appointment for the following morning was made, when more food would be required.

"I repaired to the cottage and soon learned from inquiries that Sir John Moffatt had been murdered and that an American gentleman was charged with the crime, had been arrested and was lying in the county jail awaiting his trial. My first impulse was to notify the proper authorities of what I had learned, but my knowledge of Indian character in Canada warned me not to be hasty when dealing with a semi-savage, be he American or Australian, for I had gathered from the black that he was a native of Australia.

"Securing a newspaper containing an account of the coroner's inquest, I made myself acquainted with all the known facts.

"I telegraphed to London and had my boxes sent down; arranged with a grocer in the town for a basket of provisions each morning, which I concealed from my landlady.

"The following day I had so far secured Jagga Jagga's confidence to ascertain that he was on the trail of the real criminal and would track him down if not interrupted or disturbed in the task. This strengthened my determination not to communicate with the authorities until the proof was complete.

"From Jagga Jagga I learned that he had traced footsteps from the spot where the crime was committed to a small church in Congo, the village in which I was stopping. There, unfortunately, the trail had been completely lost.

"Informing Mrs. Fenshaw that I contemplated examining the scenery in the neighborhood, I arranged with Jagga Jagga to accompany me to the scene of the tragedy. We made our way thither by a route through byways and copses. Once on the spot, he pointed out, first in the moist earth in the brushwood, behind the great oak, the impression made by the heel of a boot, on which one of the nails had been turned over at the head in driving it in. This mark, though perfectly distinct in the moist ground, left a trace imperceptible on the hard earth, save to the acute eye of the Australian, who distinguished it at a glance from others; for the place had been visited by great numbers of people since the murder.

"Jagga Jagga pointed out where Sir John had fallen on the rocks below, and then he assayed making his descent sheer over the cliff, which is nearly perpendicular. The task was full of peril, but was finally accomplished. On a ledge of rock, some twenty feet above where the body struck, Jagga Jagga found this paper."

The paper was handed to the clerk of the court. It read as follows:—

"Sir John,—
If you will meet me, alone, under the great oak, on the shelving rock, on Tuesday afternoon, at three o'clock, I can give you proofs so that your son can get a divorce from his wife. My price for the secret is two hundred pounds in gold, which you must bring with you. It will be left for you to pay or not when you have heard the story.
An Old Friend."

When the letter was read Mr. Webster requested Miss Jahns to proceed with her evidence.

"After securing the paper, which Jagga Jagga insisted in retaining in his possession for some reason, we started on our return journey, following the peculiar marked footprints, which for miles led us through bypaths and fields, always avoiding the highway. In a low piece of clay ground, in which stagnant water had stood, the imprint was surprisingly distinct. These impressions Jagga Jagga had carefully preserved by covering them with flat stones. One which had dried he dug around and under and brought it with him, lest it should be destroyed. I have it here."

She then carefully opened a small package and placed before the astonished court the footprint in clay, and pointed out to the judge and jury the mark left by the tell-tale nail.

"At the church door, to which the trail had led, the black pointed out on an oaken step many of the same peculiar indentations, where they can be found at the present time. Day after day the faithful fellow continued his search. Again I attempted to secure the letter, and at last he consented to part with it. Then I told him that his master would be convicted and hanged, but this announcement only elicited the remark that he would kill the other man and then master would be free. It required great patience to make him comprehend that killing the other man would not save his master, and that the guilty party must be pointed out, seized and taken to court. When I almost despaired of success he came to me one morning, his face beaming with satisfaction, and showed me a pair of boots. (It should be remembered that I only saw him each morning; where he spent his nights I could never ascertain). One of the boots he put on and then stamped upon the ground. It was the boot that had made the imprint at the scene of the murder and also at the church door. This was only three days since. I begged of him to give me the boot and point out its owner, but he refused, saying that he would be here at the trial and have the owner of the boots with him. Yesterday I questioned him regarding the place and time of the trial, and found that he had spent many nights under the jail wall, looking in vain for some sign from his master. I have not seen him since. I waited until the last moment, hoping that he would appear, and then tendered my evidence."

A murmur ran around the court-room when Rue Jahns ceased speaking.

Then the crier called, "Jagga Jagga! Jagga Jagga!"

A minute after loud cries and savage oaths resounded through the court-room, followed by a desperate struggle on the back benches. I heard Jagga Jagga's voice pitched in notes of triumph, and mingling with them a voice which sounded strangely familiar, and yet I could not recall where I had before heard it.

The tip staves rushed upon the disturbers, the multitude shouted. Out of the seething mass came Jagga Jagga and a white man locked in a deadly struggle, which only terminated when the officers of the court had dragged them into the space directly in front of the judge. Once on his feet my black friend gave a yell of triumph and the next instant bounded into the prisoner's box beside me, throwing his arms about my neck and uttering plaintive grunts of supreme satisfaction. Jagga Jagga was finally removed to a seat beside Rue Jahns.

The man with whom the struggle took place had regained his feet. He was venerable in appearance, with long iron-grey hair sweeping his shoulders and a clerical look prevaded his dress. There was something startling in its familiarity about the man and yet I could not call him by name. Suddenly it flashed upon me. The man was Jess Hibbard, my old-time companion in captivity in the Australian bush. He saw my look of recognition and a faint smile for a moment ran over his lips.

The court was called to order and Jagga Jagga placed in the witness box, after he had gone to the back of the court-room and returned with a large parcel.

Mr. Webster essayed an examination of the black, but in vain. Then he was left to his own devices.

Pointing at Hibbard he said, "He kill em. Master no hurt any manee. Love old manee John very much. He wear em boots," and out of the parcel came the boots; the one with the turned nail being held up and pointed out triumphantly.

"He write em paper." Then he demanded the letter of Miss Jahns. It was produced by the court and handed to the black, who in turn brought out a large, thin account book from his package, turned over the leaves until he came to a page, one half of which had been torn out, leaving a serrated edge, into which the edge of the letter written to Sir John exactly fitted, thus completing the chain of evidence.

Hibbard, who had watched the proceedings without a muscle of his face moving, spoke up in a clear, firm voice, "My Lord, the prisoner at the bar is innocent. I pushed Sir John Moffatt over the cliff. Do your worst."

Ten minutes later I was a free man and Jess Hibbard occupied the cell which I had vacated.

I clasped Rue Jahns' hand and poured out my thanks. Tom Moffatt congratulated me, while Jagga Jagga capered and leaped about the court-room like one demented. We proceeded to the Red Lion Hotel and over a substantial dinner discussed the revelations brought out by the wonderful black tracker, from whom I elicited the following additional facts:—

When he had traced the footprints to the little

church in Congo the trail was lost, but a careful examination of the church proved that the person sought was a frequent visitor there, as the mark was not only imprinted upon the oak steps outside, on the floor within, but in the pulpit itself—for Jagga Jagga had found an entrance by a window. For three Sundays every footstep to and from the church was scrutinized, with no result. On the fourth Sunday, while hiding behind a convenient hedge, the black saw Hibbard approaching the church. He recognized him at the first glance. When he had passed, the black examined his footprint. It was not the one so long sought; but your Australian black tracker can follow and distinguish any footprint, even that of a naked foot. When the services were over and the congregation dispersed, Jagga Jagga took up Hibbard's trail and followed it to a small farmhouse, half a mile beyond the village, where he caught sight of his man. That night he shadowed the house, and the next morning followed Hibbard to the church, where he remained for several hours. When he departed the black entered by a window and carefully examined the vestry. In a closet he discovered a suit of clothes, splashed with mud, and the boots so long sought. Not content he pried open a desk containing a number of papers and found a book, which recorded the names of the members of the congregation and the various sums paid by them for the maintenance of the chapel.

From the back of the book part of a blank leaf had been torn out. The quick eye of the black saw that the space was similar in size to the note written to Sir John and found on the rocks. Taking out the note he fitted it into its place—it was the final link in the chain. The boots and the book were confiscated, and from that hour he never lost sight of the place where Hibbard could be found. At night, with his ear at the keyhole of the cottage door, he had heard Hibbard order the servant to have breakfast early, as he was going to the county town to hear the trial the next day. Thither the black had followed him, but an hour was lost in getting into the court-room as it was crowded to suffocation. When his name was called he had seized Hibbard.

While Sir Thomas (for he had inherited the title) and Jagga Jagga were enjoying a smoke Rue told me, in brief terms, her history from the date of my visit to La Rue's Mills down to our meeting. In the morning she departed for Congo *en route* for London, where she proposed remaining for several months, and where I promised to pay her a visit.

She had grown into a beautiful and fascinating woman, with a soul full to maturity of charms which had so won me in our first meeting.

After her departure Tom and I went down to Moffatt Manor, but the sunlight had gone out of the dear old place in the death of Sir John. Tom tried in vain to rally his drooping spirits. Little Hazel was wild with joy over the return of her black friend, but soon grew tired and fell asleep in his arms. Something about the child alarmed me—she too had drooped and faded under the terrible ordeal. I saw that poor Tom had detected the change, as he frequently cast an anxious look upon her.

On a day, which I shall never forget, Hazel fell ill, gradually she grew worse and on the second day lay in a raging fever. Strong men falter in battle but the change which came over Tom cannot be described. An ashen pallor hung on his face, his hands and knees trembled as if stricken with the palsy, his voice sank into a hoarse whisper, and within twenty-four hours he aged in appearance fully ten years. He was blind and deaf to the outer world; every faculty was centred upon his darling. Day by day and night by night he sat by her bedside gazing in a mute and pathetic way upon her little face. When she moaned the iron of despair entered his soul. Such untiring devotion, such boundless love I have never seen in woman, much less in a man. The tie which bound him to earth was little Pet—as he loved to call her. That tie broken I shuddered at the consequences. I knew him as one with sympathies as broad and deep as ever pulsated in human breast. On the seventh night I crept softly into the chamber wherein the sick child lay, the clock just striking the hour of midnight. As I entered Hazel was sleeping, with a smile upon her flushed face. Tom sat by the bedside holding her thin, white hand. The perfume of roses came in through the open window. The light was dim and yet I saw, lying on the counterpane a large photograph, yellow and faded. A glance told me it was of the child's mother.

An awesome stillness filled the room. The flushed face of the sleeping child, the bowed head of the father, the faded, pale and ghostlike shade of the mother made a picture of the past and present full of pathos. The mother dead and not dead; dead to her husband and child, absent and yet present, silent and yet speaking in words of unutterable sadness and sorrow of the buried past. One by one the tears dropped from Tom's eyes and fell upon the little hand.

Seating myself, I spoke not a word. Out in the sky blazed a myriad of constellations with the Great Bear hanging athwart a patch of blackened cloud—symbol of unending steadfastness. I sat silent and motionless, face to face with the tragedy of two ruined lives, confronting a struggle between life and death. I knew the crisis had come. The very air was pregnant with a solemn warning, felt but unseen. Little Pet moaned and turned uneasily and then opened her eyes. A great change came over her, the flush on her cheeks died out, her eyes shone with a metalic lustre. Making a sign to her father, Tom placed the pillows behind her. Half recumbent, she gazed around with an air of childish wonderment, as if unconscious of our presence. The next moment her gaze fell upon the photograph, which she attempted to reach. Tom took it up and placed it in her little hand. Long and earnestly she gazed upon it, and then said in a voice very low, "What a beautiful woman."

Tom turned deadly pale.

"Who is she, papa?" queried the child.

With a half-choked sob Tom turned an imploring glance upon me, and then said in a hoarse whisper, "Dear little Pet, that is your mother."

The effect was instantaneous. With both little hands she held the portrait before her, turned it from side to side, then kissed and re-kissed it with a passionate tenderness which filled my eyes with tears.

Turning to her father, she said, "Where is my

mother? I want to see my mother. I'm so tired and I'm going away."

A great sob broke from Tom—the only answer.

Again she said, "Where is my dear, dear mother?"

Between half-choking sobs and in accents of anguish Tom answered, "I do not know."

"She is not dead," persisted the child, "for I can see her."

"No," sobbed Tom, "she is not dead. She has gone away."

"Why did she go?" queried little Pet.

"I cannot tell," was the broken answer.

"Don't cry, papa," whispered the child, stretching out her arms and clasping them about her father's neck, kissing him with a fondness full of pathos.

The photograph had fallen with the face upturned upon the bosom of little Pet. With wondering eyes she gazed first upon the face of her mother and then upon her father at her side, and then said softly, "Dear papa, dear mamma."

Gradually her arms relaxed and she sank back upon the pillows, with eyes half-closed, murmuring in a voice full of sweetness and tenderness, "I see my dear mamma. Good-bye, papa. I must go and find my mother."

Little Pet was dead.

BOOK VIII.

HIBBARD'S CONFESSION.

A few days after little Pet was laid away, I received the following letter:—

London.

Dear Mr. Martyne,—

Enclosed please find my cheque for the money which you sent to me through Squire Mallory. He has kept your secret well, but I guessed it long ago. I shall never forget your kindness to a poor Canadian waif, who owes to your generosity any success she may have achieved. I have received a commission from Sir Charles Tupper to paint some pictures of Canadian scenery, and shall, in consequence, sail for Canada to-day, where I hope to have the pleasure of meeting you in the near future.

Your sincere friend,

Rue Jahns.

I was dumbfounded. With all my precautions the artist had divined my secret. I would have proceeded immediately to London, but, as Rue had sailed, the step was of no avail.

The day following I determined to pay Jess Hibbard a visit at the county jail.

When ushered into the prison I found Hibbard confined in the cell occupied by me for four weeks. My old companion in the desert received me with the stoical unconcern which had characterized his conduct in the past.

"Well, Hibbard," I said, "why did you abandon me in the desert?"

"Because I gave you up for dead. I tried to rouse you, but failed, though your heart continued to beat. I took the gold, but left your share of the provisions—more precious than gold. I knew that every moment was vital, and to save my life I departed."

"How did you make your escape from the desert," I asked.

"By journeying two days directly east, where I struck kangaroo country. In two months I was on the Murray River, and from there I made my way to Sydney, from whence I sailed to England."

"As you have confessed that you threw Sir John over the cliff, have you any objection to giving the reason?"

"Not in the least," he replied, "but in doing so I must give you the history of my life, which I ask you not to divulge until after my death, which is not far distant," he said, with a grim smile.

I gave a promise not to reveal his secret, when he proceeded.

"I was born in this country. My parents were in poor circumstances, my father being employed upon an estate as gamekeeper. At an early age I began poaching on neighboring estates and disposing of the game to a butcher in a large town, who paid me paltry sums, which I spent with companions at the ale-house. My depredations were on a small scale and attracted but little attention, until I made the acquaintance, in this very town, of a youth by the name of Majeroni. He was visiting a rich aunt, but was sorely pressed for spending money. We became confidants. He suggested poaching on a large scale. I was to secure confederates and ship the game to a person in London, whom he named. For a time the plan succeeded. With another young man we devastated many adjoining estates. One night the gamekeepers came upon us suddenly. In the darkness and confusion several shots were fired, and a gamekeeper seriously wounded. I was captured, but my two companions escaped. Sir John Moffatt, upon whose preserves the affair took place, exhausted every means in his power to secure my conviction. Though I did not fire the shot I was convicted and transported for life to Western Australia. I could have made my escape from the transport ship while lying in Liverpool and secured passage to America had I possessed twenty pounds. I got a letter sent to Majeroni to that effect, but as he had inherited a fortune from his aunt he denied ever having known any such person. My life as a ticket-of-leave man you already know. With the gold which we dug I returned to England. At Liverpool I fell into low company, gambled and drank until the greater portion was lost. Several times I visited my birth-place. My father and mother were both dead and the few remaining inhabitants who had known me in my youth failed to recognize in Hezekiah Lockwood (my assumed name), Jess Hibbard the poacher and felon. You will be surprised when I inform you that I always had an inclination to preach. I know that my life did not warrant such a step, but it was impossible for me to attend a revival meeting without the conviction that

I should become a member of the Church and renounce my ways. The multitude, were they cognizant of my character, would cry out hypocrite. The charge would in part be true, but principally false. My reformation would have been complete but for two factors. I hated Sir John Moffatt with a malignant hatred which never died out. I nursed it in the chain-gang at Freemantle, I bore it through my ticket-of-leave life, carried it into the Australian desert and brought it to England. He had consigned me to the criminal class, made me an outcast, and I panted for revenge. A life of respectability for a few months always drove me to the other extreme with boon companions. When I found my resources nearly exhausted I returned to my native town as Hezekiah Lockwood, and announced that many years previous my parents had emigrated from the country to Canada (the name had at one time been a common one) and the imposition was comparatively easy. I purchased a small holding on the outskirts of the village, which yielded sufficient for my support, became a constant attendant at the chapel services, was chosen class-leader and finally became a local preacher. For months my life was in unison with my profession, but the spell came upon me. I went to a distant seaport, plunged for two weeks into vice, returned, repented, and settled down again. I was like unto a periodical drunkard, and the time came again and again when I must have excitement. I believe that had my life depended upon it I could not have resisted the inclination. I felt a supreme satisfaction in the knowledge that were my real name known all of my parishioners, who were devoutly turning up their eyes, would turn them up in holy horror. Some two months since I met Majeroni in the village and soon ascertained that he was here settling some business transaction connected with the estate of his aunt. He failed to recognize me, so I shadowed him, determined to extort money, for my available funds were at a low ebb. At first he denied ever having known Jess Hibbard, but finally made a half-acknowledgement. He gave me a ten-pound note, but this only whetted my appetite for more. He intimated that he could put a large sum in my way, and finally informed me that his sister was the wife of Tom Moffatt and that she was extremely anxious to obtain possession of her child—a little girl at the manor house. For her abduction she was willing to pay a handsome sum. As I knew the woods and every bypath, the task would be an easy one for me. Five hundred pounds would be paid for the job. Majeroni and his sister would be off the coast in a steam yacht, to which the child, after being seized, would be conveyed. I reconnoitred the manor, taking care not to meet Sir John; in fact, I never met him after my return, until the fatal day at the cliff. When my conscience rose up against me, I consoled myself by the plea that I was merely transferring the child from her father to her mother. Majeroni, during the discussions of our plans, stated that the paramount desire of Sir John was to obtain evidence against his wife to enable Tom to secure a divorce, marry again, and thus secure a male heir for the title. As the time set grew near, I fell into a state full of foreboding. I was warned again and again to abandon the project. But for my hatred of Sir John I should have given up the venture. The five hundred pounds lured me on until a great fear fell upon me, so great, that I determined to abandon the projected crime. My cupidity had been aroused. I longed for money for another debauch; so it was I hit upon an expedient which would ease my conscience and at the same time yield me funds. Then I wrote the fatal letter, picked up by the nigger on the rocks. My scheme was to inform Sir John that an attempt was on foot to kidnap the child, and confirm it by pointing out Majeroni and his sister when they came ashore at the great oak to receive the child, which they were to do on my displaying a signal from that point that I had the girl. Sir John arrived at the appointed time with the bag of sovereigns. I told him my story and pointed out the yacht lying off the coast. He consented to pay the money the moment I brought him face to face with his son's wife. I was about to give the signal, when he suddenly cried out, 'I have it at last. I recognize you—you villian. You are the wretch who shot my gamekeeper.' The words were only uttered, when I seized him by the throat. On the impulse of the moment—to save myself from prison and disgrace—I flung him over the cliff. The bag of gold lay at my feet. I picked it up and dropped it immediately when I saw a man not a dozen yards away. I darted into the bushes. You were that man. The rest of the story you know, save this, that your name, when given in connection with the charge of murder, gave me a shock, from which I never recovered. I abandoned you for dead in the desert. I robbed you of your gold. You suddenly appeared before me a moment after I had murdered Sir John Moffatt.

Strive as I might, I could not rid myself of the thought that my fate was sealed, and through your instrumentality I should be found out. I sincerely prayed for your acquittal at the coroner's inquest. Day and night you haunted me. I felt that I must be present at your trial, though prudence said, fly from England while yet there is time. A chain rooted me to the earth. A hundred times I strove to depart, but in vain. From the time I entered the court house I was fully determined at the last moment to save you. I would wait until the verdict was given. If 'not guilty,' then my lips would be sealed. If 'guilty,' I knew that I must speak."

Hibbard paused, and then said, "I only ask you not to reveal my name until after my death."

I promised and we parted.

Three days after I read in the *Times*, in London, that Hezekiah Lockwood, the self-confessed murderer of Sir John Moffatt, had been found dead in his cell. A *post-mortem* examination revealed the cause—a poison extracted from a weed found in Australia.

There arose before me that memorable morning, when I found that our horses were dead on the confines of the desert. Did he gather the fatal weed at that time? Only the Infinite could answer the question. The man belonged to a type not frequently met with, strong in passions, resolute in endeavor, swayed by impulses for bad which he struggled to overcome, but with only partial success.

Hibbard was not a hypocrite, and yet he played the part of one with consummate success. The conflict in his soul between right and wrong must have been continuous and intense. The battle had been lost, but not without a struggle. It was not death, but life which he dreaded, and, if the human body be the basis of the mind, he must have found himself constantly menaced by terrors the many dream not of. His life was not purely physical, and in many ways his career was the result of fortuitous variations acting upon a combination of good and evil blended in the individual.

In judging the man I felt that justice demanded that I should "hear the other side," but no echo came from the tomb, and Hibbard passed away execrated as an impostor and murderer who died a coward.

BOOK IX.

RUE'S LIFE.

Three days after her triumph in the Salon Rue sat in her little room in Rome with crossed arms and bowed head. She had been ill; prostrated by the re-action following the completion of the great painting. Not a whisper of her success had reached her, and in her own heart she abandoned all hope.

A tap at the door.

Then there entered a gentleman, who enquired, "Miss Jahns?"

"Yes," she answered.

"The painter of 'The Triumph of the Martyrs?'"

"The painter," was her reply.

"In behalf of the Order, in behalf of humanity, permit me to congratulate you, Miss Jahns. You have won a great triumph, you have perpetuated heroism, you have taught the world a mighty lesson. I can say no more. What the value of your work is, I cannot tell. That it is immense, all who have seen it agree. I have hastened from Paris to purchase it; not for myself, but for the purpose of presenting it to the Order. My offer is one hundred thousand francs; much less than its intrinsic value, but all that my purse will allow."

Rue gazed upon the man wonderingly. Had he gone mad? No; it was all real. She had triumphed at last. The tears dropping from her eyes were full of rest and thankfulness. Then she made answer, "If the painting is for the Jesuits, it is yours. They have been very kind to me, and they died for the poor red men of my native land, Canada.

One month later Rue took the train, *en route* for London, where she purposed remaining a few months ere she returned to Canada.

The compartment was empty when she entered, but she was immediately followed by a lady dressed in deep mourning. Ere they had reached Florence, Rue had learned that her companion was a young English widow. Her husband had died a few months previous in Egypt, where he held a position. Mrs. Cooper was going direct to London, where her brother would meet her. The result was a mutual agreement that they would make the entire journey together, which they did.

On arriving in London, at the Langham, Mrs. Cooper found a letter from her brother, announcing that he would be detained in France for a month, and advising her to take lodgings in the city until his return. This she decided to do; suggesting to Rue the desirability of her doing the same during her stay. They secured apartments near the Strand, and spent the days in visiting the galleries.

After two week's time Mrs. Cooper suggested a run down to the Dover coast, where she owned a small estate. The view from the sea was most charming, and now that her friend was an artist she had set her heart upon having a sketch made which at a later date would become a painting. She had ample means and would cheerfully pay any sum. Rue consented; but their departure was delayed from day to day on the plea that a steam yacht must be secured to convey them to the point where the view was the most charming. Finally they ran down to a small station near the coast on the morning train, lunched and drove across the country for ten miles to Fishport. The yacht was lying off the harbor, but on a signal sent a boat ashore for Mrs. Cooper and Rue; embarking, they were laughing and chatting gaily when Rue glanced casually at one of the rowers whose head was covered with a broad-brimmed straw hat drawn so as to conceal his face. She started; the contour of the form was familiar. At that instant the breeze lifted the hat for a moment. There could be no doubt, it was Majeroni, disguised as an ordinary seaman. She turned to Mrs. Cooper, when suddenly it came upon her that there was a marked resemblance between Majeroni and the woman, between whom a significant look flashed. "I insist upon being taken ashore at once, Mrs. Cooper," Rue exclaimed. "I shall not go on board the yacht." Mrs. Cooper did not answer, but at a sign given by Majeroni the rowers redoubled their efforts. A boat going in the opposite direction shot by. Suddenly, and without a word of warning, Rue sprang into the sea. What followed has been described in a previous book, from which it is evident that the plan to kidnap Hazel had been concocted by Majeroni for the purpose of securing the co-operation of his sister in inveigling Rue upon the yacht. From the time of her refusal Majeroni had kept a strict watch upon Rue, and before leaving had summoned his sister to take his place.

A spy had informed Mrs. Moffatt of Rue's coming departure. The apparent accidental meeting in the railway train and the journey to Fishport, were all parts of a plan to induce Rue to visit Majeroni's yacht, where she would have been completely at his mercy, as it was his intention to steam away to the northern ports of Africa the moment he secured the prize.

BOOK X.

TO CANADA.

Tom came up to London for a day previous to my sailing for New York. Our parting was a sad one; but I got a promise that in the early fall he would pay me a visit. Once inside Sandy Hook I was impatient to visit the little office in which I had held the memorable interview with my first and only client.

Mounting the rickety stairs, I found the room door wide open and the place occupied by a new-fledged lawyer who was waiting for a client. He had been in possession continuously from my departure, having leased the office the next day. No person resembling Billa La Rue had ever called and enquired for Carl Martyne. At the bank in Wall Street the same answer was returned. The proceeds of the gold had accumulated into a considerable sum, subject to my check. I had not heard from Rue, and on the second day I determined to proceed to La Rue's Mills.

Jagga Jagga and I stepped from the train at Mallorytown a sunny morning in September, and, knapsack in hand strolled down the river road, making our way to the residence of the fat woman who had given me the weird history of Billa La Rue. Leaving my black friend to amuse himself on the river, I stepped into the path leading by the old rifle-pits and under the whispering Lombardy poplars, mused as I went slowly forward. An impulse led me onward to my fate, for the die was cast, I was powerless, drifting with the impassioned tide born of love for Rue Jahns. I made my way directly to the tomb of Billa La Rue beneath the widespreading chestnut, amid whose branches the descendants of Chitter and Rosa disported themselves.

As I drew near I saw curled up on the great tombstone a bundle of white muslin with the tip of a shoe peeping out of one fold and a tangled mass of yellow hair streaming from beneath a broad hat. I went forward on the velvety grass on tip-toe, intending a surpise, but found that Rue Jahns was fast asleep. I caught a glimpse of her face, over which a smile flitted. The long lashes falling upon her berry brown cheeks twitched convulsively and momentarily I expected to see her eyes open. She was dreaming and this was her dream.

Rue's Dream.

"I was in a balloon, swinging backward and forward in space, but tethered by a single silken cord to the earth beneath. Suddenly the cord snapped and *he* was by my side. The stars were shining above, while beneath rolled great oceans of mist, evolving gigantic mountains and moorlands, through which shot gleams of light. The gentle, swaying motion of the car was rhythmatic with the thought that æons of time I had thus floated through space.

"A sigh, faint as ever fell upon human ear, recalled me to the present.

"The blackness of night grew less intense, a purple mist enveloped *us*, the dark clouds rolled away one by one; gleams of light shot through the circling, eddying vapors. The sun, like a great ball of fire, came forth, and it was day. *He* looked into my eyes and smiled, which said, 'I am happy.' Not a word was spoken, a gleam of the eye, a pressure of the hand, told in language more eloquent than tongue can utter our supreme content.

"Below us lay the great Pacific Ocean, gleaming and glinting in the morning sun. The variegated flying fish sprang from the crests of the waves, flashed away for a brief time, then sank into the heaving blue.

"The car swayed with a gentle undulating motion in unison with our blended souls. Hand clasped hand and we were happy.

"The morning wind blew fresh and strong, the surges rejoiced as they broke into white crests and laughed with glee in their freedom and their play. The albatross, on pinions more flexible than steel, floated through the azure blue, seeming to defy all laws of nature, measuring league upon league without the movement of a wing, to me the emblem of eternal motion, the sign of our passion—bliss; for hand clasped hand and we were happy.

"Over coral islands we floated, islands green with palm and fern, whereon the children of nature sported, as the red deer sports in the forest; islands with blue-topped mountains, shaded valleys, babbling streams and grass thatched huts—islands where all who love are free, and, as hand clasped hand, I murmured, 'We are happy.'

"Away out on the bosom of the deep rested a little cloud—a frown upon the face of mother ocean. It kissed the waves and blackened them, as the kiss of lust blackens the lips of innocence. Forked lightning leaped forth as the snake darts its venomous tongue; the wind moaned and sighed like a lost soul driven from the gates of Paradise; and yet hand clasped hand and we were happy.

"We heard the Storm King on his deadly march, as he licked up the billows and hurled the trembling waters into foam. We saw the flash, and bent our ears to the cannonade of the very elements, struggling, fighting for supremacy. The black pall of a cyclone encompassed us, tossing our frail car like an air-bubble, and beating us down to the jaws of death yawning beneath; but hand clasped hand and we were happy.

"Seized by the demon of destruction, we dashed through the billows. The salt sea foam kissed our cheeks and cried, 'Welcome! Welcome!' as we raced like a meteor by the angry waves, heeding not, caring not, for hand clasped hand and we were happy.

"We heard the breakers beating their funereal drum; on the rock-bound coast where gallant tars had plunged to death. We caught glimpses of the beacon light, whose every ray cried, 'Beware! Beware!' We saw beneath, a gallant ship, with faces upturned and white with fear, lest we perished; but hand clasped hand and we were happy.

"In fiendish glee the hurricane cast us into the seething waters, then lifted us high into the air, as if mocking at our helplessness, then with a shriek threw us into a crescent of sand; but in the supreme moment when, consciousness departed, hand clasped hand and we were happy."

PLUM HOLLOW.   251

As I watched the smile on Rue's face, an irresistible impulse came upon me. I stooped down and kissed her on the cheek. She sprang to her feet and exclaimed, "How dare you?"

"Because I love you," I answered boldly.

She spoke not a word, but knelt down and from under the great stone brought forth a gold coin. As she held it up I saw that it was similar to the coins given to me by my first client: the missing coin, for one had been lacking.

Then Rue said slowly, "When the dear old man came out of the hills with the iron box, he gave me this, and bade me hide it under the tomb, there to remain until someone came here and asked me to go out into the world with him, when I was to give him the coin and my hand. You have come; here is the coin and this the hand."

BOOK XI.

THE WEDDING DAY.

Our wedding day had come. We were to be married under the great chestnut, beside the last resting-place of Billa La Rue. A bright September morning, with here and there a leaf turning to gold, the birds flitting from branch to branch, the squirrels scampering on the brown grass. A large marquee tent, in which the *dejenuer* was spread, was the centre of attraction for Jagga Jagga, who sniffed the viands with evident satisfaction.

The first guest to arrive was the fat woman from up the river, who, amid gasps and puffs, announced that she had brought her son because he played on the "fiddle." Then came Dan Polly and his sister Sally, hand in hand, arrayed in their Sunday best, beaming with satisfaction and grateful because Rue had forgiven the past. Rue, accompanied by Jahns *pater* and her step-mother, next appeared. Jahns' knee breeches and dress coat, with the silver buckles of his pointed shoes, contrasted with Mrs. Jahns' new black silk and ample kerchief, made a picture never to be forgotten. Mr. Wood, Mr. Percy and Dr. Lane drove up in a smart turn-out, followed by fisherman Thompson, of Grenadier Island, and his entire family on foot. Squire Mallory, with his long white locks and his genial smile, came ambling in on his favorite pony. Then there was a pause, succeeded by a rattling of wheels, as into the sunlight there flashed a barouche, gaily decorated with ribbons. The driver, mine host Armstrong, beaming with good nature and pointing his whip at the occupants of the carriage, the Witch of Plum Hollow and the erratic doctor. While they were alighting, a light carriage dashed up at a speed which threatened to overturn the entire party, and out jumped Tom Moffatt.

The last arrival made my happiness complete. Ten minutes later we greeted the clergyman. In half an hour the knot was tied, the pines on the hill chanting the wedding march and the great river whispering a benediction. Jagga Jagga saluted the bride and received a kiss in return, a favor which made me half-jealous.

The spirits of the guests rose with the popping of the champagne corks (mine could mount no higher). Jahns' *pater* passed by rapid transitions from the shrinking recluse into the polite and polished gentleman of long ago, his *bon mots* and sallies of wit provoking hilarious laughter. The Witch caught the infection and engaged the doctor in a duel of wit. In the midst of the merriment the violin struck up. Tom Moffat, with a courage for which I never gave him credit, made a vain attempt to encircle the waist of the fat woman as they whirled in a waltz. The doctor led Mrs. Jahns out, Jahns *pater* took for his partner the Witch, while I, contrary to all precedent, danced with my wife. The remainder of the party joined in the fun. Soon we were all whirling on the crisp grass in knots and tangles and confusion. The spirit of revelry urging us on until the woods resounded with our laughter and the tomb of Billa La Rue kept time with our beating footsteps.

FATE OF MAJERONI.

Some fifteen months after our marriage I received a copy of the *Melbourne Argus* from Fred White, of Adelaide, containing the following:—

"We learn from the captain of a schooner engaged in the South Pacific trade that for several months past a steam yacht has been cruising about, visiting New Britain, New Ireland and the Admiralty Isles. She was commanded by her owner, Signor Majeroni, who was accompanied by his sister, Mrs. Moffatt. On January 21st, during a heavy gale, the yacht went ashore at Isabel Island, one of the Salomon group.

"Whether the captain and crew were drowned or reached the land is not known. In either case their fate is sealed as the natives of this group are the most ferocious cannibals south of the line.

"It will be remembered that it was at the Salomon Isles that the commodore of the British fleet in these seas lost his life a few years since, being shot with poisoned arrows.

"The High Commissioner at Thursday Island will dispatch a man-of-war to the scene, but the captives (if they escaped from the sea) will have been eaten long before any vessel can reach the group."

FINIS.

Publisher's Notice.

We have purchased from Mr. Thad. W. H. Leavitt the Canadian copyright for his forthcoming novel, "Cooee."

This book is a pen picture of the Australian Republic in the Thirtieth century. It will be found replete with interest, depicting as it does, the physical, moral and intellectual status of a people whom the author depicts as having been isolated for ten centuries.

The marvellous advance in the arts and sciences, government, educational aids and the development of thought, combine in creating a work of intense interest.

THE WELLS PUBLISHING CO.,
TORONTO.

IN PRESS . . .

"COOEE"

A Realistic Novel of Australia in the 30th Century

BY

THAD. W. H. LEAVITT

CPSIA information can be obtained
at www.ICGtesting.com
Printed in the USA
LVOW04*0805031216
515646LV00006B/52/P

9 781296 609863